CAT LADY CHRONICLES

Officina Libraria srl
via Romussi 4
20125 Milan, Italy
www.officinalibraria.com

Graphic Design
Paola Gallerani

Editing
Yarwood Editorial Services

Colour Separation
Eurofotolit, Cernusco sul Naviglio (Milan)

Printed in Italy by
Monotipia Cremonese (Cremona)
in the month of July 2012
ex Officina Libraria Jellinek et Gallerani

isbn: 978-88-89854-98-3

Diane Lovejoy

Cat Lady CHRONICLES

with 12 original drawings of the 10 original
Lovejoy cats by Gabriella Gallerani

OFFICINA
LIBRARIA

CONTENTS

Inseparable

*C*at Lady! Cat Lady! Cat Lady! I always smile when the owner of my neighborhood nail salon greets me in this effusive way. She knows that I answer also to this name, even though her little black book indicates, "Diane L., mani–pedi, 6:00 p.m."

The Vietnamese women working at the salon in Houston barely speak English, but they have learned a few basics and enjoy teasing me about my feline obsessions. Whenever I arrive for my standing appointment at Instyle Nails, the salonistas ask, "Cat Lady, do you have kids?" To which I coyly reply, "That depends on your definition of kids."

Let me begin this true story by disclosing the head count at home. I have ten cats. I did not set out with a charter in hand, emboldened to rescue and adopt so many orphaned felines. Nor did I dream that I, a self-contained, deferential person, would step far outside of my comfort zone and ultimately denounce veterinary authority, all in the name of cats.

This is a coming-of-age story, but it is not exclusively about cats who advance from being frisky kittens to the feline equivalent of senior citizens. This is my story, too, only I wasn't so young when I began my journey, guided by a hyperactive sixth sense for attracting stray felines. Yet I made up for lost time and quickly became someone who could not live without cats, and I am certain they feel the same about me. Their unconditional love fuels my unconventional lifestyle. Thankfully, my husband, Michael, endorses my being Cat Lady; in fact, he cheered me on. And once I revved up, I went full bore.

This is not to imply I have no life outside of "Catland," our self-named feline compound where we cohabitate with Lucius, Lydia, Leo, Linus, L.B., and Alvar; and where our garage apartment—or "guest quarters," as realtors like to say—is occupied by Lillie, T.J., Perkins, and Miss Tommie. I have worked for more than thirty years as an editor of museum publications and art books, and my vocation and my avocation as Cat Lady were not intertwined initially. I was on a fast learning curve, balancing the immutable deadlines and multiple responsibilities of my profession with the insistent demands of a codependent life with ten felines.

Born This Way

How did I go from zero to ten, becoming a connoisseur of cats? I have wondered if a baby girl enters the world predestined to be a Cat Lady. While consulting a family scrapbook, I discovered a faded black-and-white snapshot of my father instructing me, as a one-year-old, in the gentle art of petting a stray cat. There I was in Jackson Square in New Orleans, my hometown, dressed in a pint-sized, personalized Tulane University "Greenie" sweatshirt and baggy corduroy pants. Perhaps this first caress of a cat sealed the deal for my future fixation.

I also found a Kodachrome slide presenting me as a curly-headed two-year-old playing with Prissy, a Siamese cat who hung out in our neighborhood. Apparently, I liked Prissy very much and looked forward to her crossing the neighbor's lawn each day to pose on the front steps of our house. But I was confused one evening when Prissy brought me an unwrapped gift, a dead bird. My mother reports that my chubby cheeks became red as I stomped my feet at Prissy for killing the bird, although I came around to forgiving the cat. Maybe Prissy already knew what was in the cards for the girl with the corkscrew curls. Is being Cat Lady in my DNA?

I grew up with my loving parents in households not only in New Orleans but also in commuter suburbs near Chicago and New York City. My father, a broadcast journalist, and my mother, who before having children was employed as a television reporter, taught me respect for the written word. My father stayed up late at nights writing documentaries, and I often fell asleep to the sound of two of his fingers pecking the typewriter keys. In keeping with their talents as writers, both of my parents were voracious readers who passed on to me their affection for books. Some of my fondest memories are of studying the eclectic publications stacked on the shelves in our homes; among the treasures were issues of the literary magazine that my mother edited during her senior year at Tulane. She took my sister, Marcy, and me as often as possible to the Maple Street Bookstore in New Orleans, where I was proud to graduate from reading in the designated children's room to buying books in the room where adults gathered and browsed. I felt like I was making a seismic statement as a teenager when I used part of my weekly allowance to purchase my first paperback novel: *The Golden Notebook* by Doris Lessing.

My parents also instilled in their children a love of animals, and our homes always included a cat and a dog. I was enamored of our Maltese, Snowy, whom I spoiled rotten, whereas Marcy catered to our tuxedo cat, Fluffy. I'm not proud to own up to this now, but I honestly don't recall paying much attention to Fluffy. When my brother, Matthew, was born, in 1970, Snowy became insanely jealous, and my father tried to explain to me that "one of the two had to go." Fluffy was never up for grabs, and, had I been paying close attention, I would have recognized instantly that cats rule.

If there is such a thing as tracing a genetic link to a relative beyond one's parents, then I probably inherited the cat-rescue gene from Aunt Susan, my father's sister. She loved cats and never thought of leaving home without them for extended periods of time. Susan traveled with her beloved Mickey, Minnie, and Lucky between her Upper West Side apartment in New York City and her weekend house in Gloucester, Massachusetts. I remember admiring her resolve to transport her cats comfortably and to give them as much of her undivided attention as possible, even though she had a demanding career as a studio executive in the recording industry. Still, nothing from my childhood or teenage years pointed to the all-consuming life I lead with three orange tabbies, three grey tabbies, three calicos, one white-and-black cat—and one husband.

A possible hint of my fascination with the feline world is that I never missed an episode of the 1960s television series *Batman,* which featured Julie Newmar as the beguiling, conniving, and whip-snapping Catwoman. Perhaps I was empowered by Catwoman, because, when I graduated from high school, I chose to enter the all-female province of Wellesley College.

Like many women who attended Wellesley during the 1970s, I had my consciousness raised there. But I was certainly not a CLOC (Cat Lady on Campus). I spent the majority of my first two years at Wellesley poring over art history books with an emphasis on the nineteenth century; writing term papers on Pre-Raphaelitism and Louis Sullivan's idea of architecture and on other specialized subjects that, as my father worriedly reminded me, were not marketable in the "real world"; and studying for exams that always included a trick question related to the feminist movement.

I pursued art history at the École du Louvre during my junior year in Paris, where I frequented the city's famous museums at every opportunity, before and after classes. And what about studying those equally famous French cats? How could I have missed seeing them on the boulevards and in the brasseries?

When I returned to Wellesley for my senior year, I was fluent in French but still not conversant in cat-world history. My trajectory did not allow for a detour, even a U-turn. So, after graduation, along with many well-intentioned art history students who had convinced their parents that they could earn a reliable living in the arts, I headed straight for Manhattan.

The old-girl network at Wellesley paid off, and I was thrilled to be hired for my first full-time professional job as a fast-typing receptionist at Sotheby's, back in the days when the IBM Selectric reigned supreme. I loved arriving for work at Sotheby's glamorous headquarters, with its storefront windows looking out on Madison Avenue, and I kept hoping that someone would mistake me for Audrey Hepburn in her Givenchy black dress playing Holly Golightly in *Breakfast at Tiffany's.* Not a chance.

I trained at the art auction house with Valerie, a lovely woman who seemed unusually attached to her cat, Miss Kitty. I didn't understand the special bond between them, so I wasn't adept at conversing with Valerie about cats, in general, and about Miss Kitty, in particular. If Valerie and I ever cross paths again, I promise to make up to her for my shortcomings.

Valerie and I compared notes on who had the tiniest apartment, and I won. I lived in a rent-controlled, 325-foot studio steps away from Sotheby's, and stray cats were nonexistent in the immaculate neighborhood that I called home. Mine was a prescribed life, one that consisted mostly of long hours during the work week. My friends from my "Sotheby's period" tell me that I always looked so serious when I was in my early twenties, trying to find my way in the art world. One socialite on staff—she wore her status well—counseled me to wear jewel tones to brighten my demeanor, which was her subtle way of saying that I looked old for my age. "Do you ever have fun?" she asked in her breathless voice.

I was determined to prove myself and to justify that my collegiate years studying art history would return benefits on my parents' investment. Eventually, I was promoted from my entry-level position to the post of chief cataloguer in the jewelry department, which, after the Impressionist paintings department, earned the highest annual income for the auction house. The seeds of my publishing career were sown at Sotheby's, where I discovered how much I liked arranging images and words on a page to tell a story. The objective of the auction catalogues was clear: Sell, Sell, Sell.

I worked closely with Sotheby's in-house publications department to produce the "highly important" and "magnificent" (the marketers' superlatives) jewelry catalogues and to coordinate the photography for the paid advertisements of the jewelry auctions that ran in the likes of *Town & Country* and *Vogue*. To an outsider looking in, my world appeared rarefied and refined. And it was. But there was also the reality of isolation: I was literally locked behind closed doors, where my desk was positioned next to the vault in which all of the valuable gems were stored.

Much of my job depended on cranking out enticing descriptions of oversized jewels and ornate baubles. Long before the job title of "webmistress" existed, I was luring Sotheby's clientele into my bejeweled web. I also was way ahead of Twitter in mandating brevity: "Glittering Rubies Encircle Canary Diamonds in Dazzling 18K Gold." Surely Holly Golightly would have approved.

Woulda, Coulda, Shoulda

My "catless" life continued for many years. I resigned from Sotheby's when I realized that I had inadvertently created my own dead end. I didn't want to become a gemologist—squinting at hallmarks, inspecting precious stones through loupes, and estimating prices for the rest of my life. Some of my Wellesley friends were getting married already, and I felt competitive. Sotheby's was staffed mostly by women, and my odds of meeting Mr. Right were slim at best. It was time to venture out of my gilded cage and return to the Midwest. My travel agent was shocked when I bought a one-way airplane ticket to Chicago. Who in her right mind would think of leaving the greatest city on earth? But I knew it was time to go.

I was excited to join the staff of the Art Institute of Chicago. As the assistant director of public relations and then the associate director of marketing services, I publicized some of the most ambitious Impressionist exhibitions of the 1980s—a game-changing decade for blockbuster art shows.

I enjoyed writing diverse materials for the public weal, reaching the Art Institute's audience of more than one hundred thousand members. Before long, I was tapped to draft the fund-raising appeals issued by the chairman of the board. I didn't have the requisite burning ambition to be the power behind the throne, but it was still nice to be close to the throne. I felt fulfilled by my work and was committed to making a difference in the art world, in my own, below-the-radar way.

I should have been looking for a cat all along, though, because I felt alone more often than not. A cat would have liked me: I was quiet, tidy, and, just like a cat, was a creature of habit. As was the case in New York, I lived in a tiny apartment, this time in a former Art Deco high-rise hotel situated in Chicago's scenic Gold Coast neighborhood. There, too, stray cats were an anomaly. A window seat in my seventeenth-floor apartment overlooked a wide expanse of Lake Michigan and also a picturesque side street lined with nineteenth-century brownstones. A cat and I could have curled up together while I edited materials for my museum work or read for sheer pleasure. But I pursued a different routine and was accustomed to coming home to an empty apartment, day after day. Cat Lady-esque tendencies had not yet overtaken me.

Watching Over Me

My professional mentor in Chicago was an unabashed cat lover. I got to know Virginia "Dinny" Butts well while interning for three summers in the editorial and features departments of the *Chicago Sun-Times* newspaper. Miss Butts, as she insisted on being properly addressed in her corporate suite, was the vice president of public relations for Field Enterprises, Inc., and she also assisted the Marshall Field family—one of Chicago's first families—in their personal public relations. Dinny was beautiful, brilliant, and charming, a woman both revered and feared for her perfection. She introduced me to her sophisticated ways of the world: St. John fashion shows at Marshall Field's flagship store on State Street; lunches at Le Perroquet, where she claimed a corner booth and the maître d' addressed her reverentially as Madame Butts; and grocery shopping at the chicest convenience mart in town. Dinny also taught me the importance of preparing a daily "to do" list, and I can still hear her singsong reminder echoing in the corridors of the cigarette smoke-filled newsroom, "Don't bury the lead!"

Dinny and I never talked explicitly about leading with the heart, yet despite her numerous career awards and professional accomplishments, I think of her best as someone who profoundly loved her husband, Dr. Jack Berger. He had contracted a rare disease in China that caused him to lose his vision. No matter her ambitions and office-related obligations, Dinny cared for Jack selflessly. She also doted on her handsome black cat, Christopher, with inspired devotion. Whenever I visited Dinny and Jack at their nearby townhome, I played with Christopher while simultaneously asking Dinny for career advice. No one could accuse me of missing a professional growth opportunity, although I was not building a sideline career searching for cats in the Windy City.

I wish that Dinny had lived long enough to see me become Cat Lady. She succumbed to cancer several years before I hit my stride, but her love of cats endures. Through a legacy gift, she established the Virginia Butts Berger Cat Clinic, a rehabilitation and treatment center at the Anti-Cruelty Society in Chicago. I imagine that Dinny is watching over me now, smiling from heaven as she observes my every move in the company of cats.

Dinny was the first person in whom I confided when I knew I was going to abandon my solitary life and marry Michael. He and I met in Chicago on a blind date orchestrated by one of his childhood friends who had married one of my Wellesley classmates. At Wellesley, I was painfully shy and avoided the Harvard and MIT "mixers" at all cost. Post-Wellesley, it took a lot of prompting from my friends to coax me to agree to a blind date.

Michael had been divorced for four years and was receptive to dating again, whereas, after numerous mismatches, I had officially given up on finding anyone compatible. Perhaps I, like many cats, had a tendency to act aloof and standoffish. I hadn't found the balance between being self-reliant and being amenable to another's affection and attention.

I can't pretend that I didn't feel sorry for myself when I spent a Saturday night reading the first edition of Sunday's *Chicago Sun-Times*. As soon as feelings of loneliness crept up on me, I remembered the blind date who pitifully explained why he was late in meeting me for an after-work cocktail: He couldn't find the Art Institute of Chicago, whose imposing, blocks-long edifice is flanked by two monumental sculptures of bronze lions. Being on my own *was* fine.

Probably because I never suspected I was being fixed up on another dreaded blind date, I agreed to give Michael a personal tour of the Art Institute. I knew

The Scoop on...

Looking Like a Cat Lady

What to wear? You may be wondering if I dress the part of the Cat Lady who doles out cups of cat food while sporting a tattered bathrobe and shuffling around the house in a pair of scruffy bedroom slippers. Even the Crazy Cat Lady Action Figure (purchasable online!) doesn't come with a change of clothes. People traditionally associate Cat Ladies with fashion victims. Can't the Cat Lady wear Prada?

The leopard look is back in vogue, although I'm not convinced it ever left the runway. As an editor, it's easy for me to relate to spot-on. Bring on the animal-inspired clothes! To drive home the point further, I could carry a Hello Kitty handbag with me wherever I go and wear a pair of Miu Miu's "leaping feline"-patterned satin slippers.

The simple truth is that I am an understated dresser. I like to wear twinsets and trousers in the fall and winter, and sleeveless shirtdresses in the spring and summer. That way, no matter the fashion season, I can avoid wardrobe malfunctions. Just as beauty is in the eye of the beholder, being a put-together Cat Lady is a state of mind.

all of the collection highlights from having led the Chicago and national and international press on numerous treasure hunts through the vast complex. Michael passed my first test when he arrived punctually, getting to the right place at the right time. This was encouraging: A seventh-generation Texan could navigate the busy streets of Chicago without a hitch. Even though I did not share his taste for the imperial objects featured in the *Suleyman the Magnificent* exhibition, we clicked on that first date and traded stories about politics and college football and Cajun cooking over a long dinner afterward. Michael was passionate about the University of Texas Longhorns, and he laughed at my unoriginal joke about Wellesley being undefeated on the gridiron since 1876. I thought we had hit a bump in the potential romantic road when Michael made it clear that he didn't care for opera, but I forgave this character flaw. Michael and I had a grand total of three dates before we stated the obvious: We were soul mates.

My parents were living in London when Michael and I announced our engagement. Because of the distance geographically, my mother could not take charge of wedding planning. I bought a 1950s gown from a vintage clothing shop managed by a Texan who had been the bridal director at Neiman Marcus in Dallas. She appreciated that I was marrying one of her kind, and, in the back room where she worked her magic with lace and tulle, she threw in some extra seed pearls for free to adorn my veil. For her wedding gift to us, she inscribed a Tex-Mex cookbook with these three words: "Follow your bliss." Little did we know that we would define our bliss by the number of felines in residence.

I moved on from shopping to coordinate all of the logistical details of our wedding, and I didn't stop there. I even insisted on writing our marital vows, and, during the dress rehearsal for our wedding, I thought I caught the justice of the peace mouthing "control freak" to his personal assistant. Michael and I wed in Chicago on a blizzard-free day in early December.

As newlyweds, we focused on our careers—his is in international business development—not on "having cats." As fate would have it, we also joined the ranks of childless couples. When we relocated to his native Houston, I was hired by the Museum of Fine Arts, where I have worked ever since as publications director, chasing delinquent author-curators, editing essays overnight, and overseeing precariously tight production schedules.

My steady routines were thrown for a loop when, twelve years ago, I found an emaciated feline in our backyard. I fell in love with the cat we eventually named Lucius and discovered that I did not subscribe to the power of one. More cats arrived. Many more followed. Many more stayed.

Secret Agent

When I embarked on my cat-rescuing mission, I was embarrassed to admit to my mounting addiction. I had always been a "good girl": I studied hard to make straight As, I didn't drink, I didn't smoke, and I didn't do drugs. I exercised fanatically at a wacky place named Women's Workout World in Chicago, but otherwise I really didn't know what it felt like to have a fiendish, got-to-kick-it habit. I was getting high from a different adrenaline. Could there be such a thing as going on a bender for adopting homeless cats?

Coincidentally, I was assigned to meet with a number of high-profile art collectors about books featuring their private holdings. Although their collections varied—from avant-garde jewelry to contemporary Asian art—the collectors all talked zealously about their desire to acquire, and I could relate. Colleagues began to catch on gradually that I was rapidly acquiring cats by the month, and they couldn't help but notice that my normally reserved self was exhilarated.

With the adoption of each feline, I worried that my seemingly uncontrollable situation at home might hinder my productivity at the office. Would fellow editors query, "Are you living a double life?" In that regard, I suppose I was no different from the classic addict who strives to keep two lives apart.

But I was seeking a new model for living, and I vowed to put my Cat Lady persona to work. I considered the qualities in cats I admired most: their impeccable grooming, their all-knowing silence, their survival-of-the-fittest instinct, their focus.

I read a corroborating article in an issue of *Office Solutions* magazine that happened to be sitting on an empty table in the museum's lunchroom. The article extolled the virtues of "working like a cat," and many of the mantras hit home: Don't let anything ruffle your whiskers, don't use your [manicured] claws except for a good reason, and, most important, don't forget that you are a lion at heart.

I was eager for the two of us to live happily ever after: the art-book editor who scrutinized relationships among words and examined affinities between artworks, and the Cat Lady who counseled ten cats to *please* get along. Soon my wish was granted. I was invited to consult on a museum exhibition about the cat in art and to develop an "artful cat" wall calendar. My reputation as Cat Lady began to precede me, and my curatorial colleagues continue to seek my nonacademic, straight-from-the-heart advice, which I dispense freely; in return, they send me cat-motif cards for every Hallmark holiday and deliver flea-market cat collectibles to my desk (it used to be that, whenever I saw the word "flea," I associated it only with the famed markets of Paris). Comments such as "thanks for the sensitive edit," and "when I die and come back to earth, I want to be one of your cats," carry equal weight in my book.

Certainly, the kitschy kitty world differs from my pristine professional environment, where I am surrounded by the highest forms of artistic expression. Nonetheless, I have found correlations and correspondences between these two worlds so that they are in sync.

A Pitch-Perfect Cat Lady

Oh, that voice, that super-squeaky one that will never be heard at Covent Garden or La Scala or at other famous opera houses of the world. I am referring, of course, to my Cat Lady voice. I am routinely embarrassed when I enter Dr. O.'s office because the always upbeat office manager addresses me in the voice she uses for speaking to cats. "Well, hello there, you've come back to see us again!" The four resident office cats greet me while the human clients waiting in the office try their best to smile indulgently. Still, I find myself responding in my equally falsetto voice, "Yes, hello, everybody, I'm back!"

Perhaps it's time to take on *The X Factor* and launch a competition to determine who among Cat Ladies has the best voice for communicating with cats. I don't mean the most soothing voice; I mean the hitting-the-high-note-out-of-the-ballpark voice. I like to warm up my vocal chords before calling Lucius, Lydia, Leo, Lillie, T.J., Perkins, Miss Tommie, Linus, L.B., and Alvar. Without fail, I also hear my inner voice speaking to me.

Term Limits

Like most employees, I respond to praise from my boss. I also was complimented in what amounted to an unofficial performance review when our cats' veterinarian, Dr. O., remarked, "You have created an ecosystem for cats." Who knew I had the ability? This is my unexpected calling. With that said, I hesitated at first to put "Cat Lady" in the title of this book because the term is fraught with unflattering, even unkind stereotypes. But I choose to focus on the flip side of the coin.

Isn't there a little bit of the Cat Lady in all of us who can't say no to a creature in need? The editor takes a red pencil to a manuscript or makes on-screen changes to text files, aiming for a bona fide assist. The hand discreetly aids the author in refining his or her true voice. The Cat Lady extends a hand to help those who technically cannot speak for themselves and articulate their desires. Perhaps the only variation on this helping-hand theme is how to characterize a "creature in need."

To me, authors and cats are in the same camp. They both need tender loving care and circumspect intervention, and they also crave attention from editors and Cat Ladies, respectively. In some case studies, the editor and the Cat Lady merge as one. Inseparable, indeed, and from ten furry creatures who helped me to feel comfortable in my own skin.

Speaking of the kids, let's go meet them now.

Chapter 2

Scared

Lucius

*I*n the beginning, there was only one cat, and I didn't have a clue.

I first met Lucy, as Michael and I hastily named the stray cat, when I arrived home from work one day in May 2000. I always enter our weather-beaten Craftsman-style house through the ornamental wrought-iron gate in the backyard, from where, on this occasion, I heard a distressing sound coming from under the house. I couldn't see anything, but I also couldn't pretend not to hear the continuous moan. I alerted Michael that I feared an animal was dying outside, and he said sternly that we could not let this happen on our watch.

I dropped my tote bag at its designated place. I had worked hard for this bag, having researched the appropriate carrier for manuscripts, trade articles, and the "to do" lists that Dinny had prescribed. She had emphasized that a professional woman is sized up quickly, from head to toe. So I invested in a black Ferragamo tote bag with the classic grosgrain ribbon accoutrement. It's not too Samsonite, and it's not too Louis Vuitton. It seemed right proportionately for an editor who stands only five feet tall and is employed at an art museum where conventional or stodgy formalities are often shunned.

Being petite sometimes has its advantages, though I had never volunteered before to inspect the cobwebby guts of our house, which dates to 1913. When I went outside again, I immediately saw an orange tabby cat with what appeared to be a cigarette burn or perhaps a BB gun wound beside the right rib that was poking out of a skeletal frame. The cat's face was emaciated, too, but expressive, with touches of white sprinkled around the aristocratically pointed nose and the whiskers.

Who Came First?

Something about Lucy's stiff stance reminded me of an image of a cat I had seen when I was an art history student at Wellesley. To this day, I remember vividly those much-anticipated moments during my freshman year when the Art 100 professor would stride onto the stage in the art center's auditorium and speak dramatically into the microphone: "May I have the first two slides, please?" The slide projectionist accepted her cue, and reproductions of two works of art filled the big screen. The opportunity to examine works of art— their similarities and their differences—was novel and exciting, and I got hooked on the visual exercise very fast.

While the cat remained immobile, random images flashed in my head and I relied on my nearly photographic memory to make a match. I recalled a slide from an American art class that featured a cat doorstop, probably from about 1930, by a folk art sculptor. The cat depicted resembled Lucy, now crouching on our wooden deck rail, too scared to jump to the ground. Were my eyes playing tricks on me, was life imitating art? Or had the artwork sprung to life as the stray cat?

Lucy suddenly became more talkative, her gravelly, pleading meow trying to tell me what was on her mind. Perhaps she was saying, "I came first, and I'm not leaving." I fed her some day-old salami, which was all that I could scrape together from the refrigerator, and left a saucer filled with low-fat milk.

Lucy ate every scrap in sight and gratefully lapped up the milk. I went about my business for the rest of the night, not thinking much about the cat and guessing she would go on her way. Early the next morning, I found myself peeking out of a curtain in the living room, curious about Lucy's whereabouts. She was on the next-door neighbor's front porch, patiently waiting on a pedestal and strategically out of sight from any would-be feline predators. I called "Luuuuu-cy," and the cat came running across the yard to our front porch. Without a plan in place, I began an informal routine of morning and evening feedings. I was so delighted to be taking care of Lucy that I brought out the bread plates from the china set Michael and I had received as a wedding gift. I hoped Lucy would appreciate my taste in porcelain and like the Limoges Rococo floral pattern I had chosen. All the while, my deadline-driven routines at the museum continued unabated.

I had just emerged from an intense period of publishing, leading up to the grand opening of the museum's new, 125,000-square-foot building. As publications director, I had hired and trained an all-female staff of five editors and five graphic designers. I wasn't discriminating against men; the best candidates for the job openings were always women. We all had our different styles for approaching work, but we got along, insulating ourselves from the drama—there are office bullies in art museums—and intrigue—wondering if a private collector would temporarily part company with a significant work and lend it to an exhibition.

I was what an organizational behavior specialist calls a "transactional leader," meaning I could delegate work efficiently, listen to my colleagues' ideas (and complaints), and set common goals for the staff to achieve. But even though I was more than the nominal head of the publications department, I still considered myself to be an editor at heart, and I wasn't willing to give up being hands on with the book projects that I found the most stimulating.

Our department had set its own record of issuing seven art books in six months, and I was preparing to attend a conference in New York to confer with publishing colleagues about partnering with the museum on the next tidal wave of projects. Because Michael and I had not officially claimed Lucy as our own, we were not thinking about how the cat would be fed during our brief absence for one weekend in June. I still feel guilty recalling our thoughtlessness. How could we have been so ignorant?

But Lucy was forgiving and also hungry, as we found the cat waiting on our front doormat when we returned. Our neighbor noticed that we were home again and told us that she and her husband had been feeding Lucy, but, given the impending birth of their first child, they could not adopt an animal at this time. Lucy knew that it was now or never. Michael felt Lucy rubbing against his leg and said "yes" on the spot, which proved to be a defining moment in our previously childless history.

Our first week as the official caregivers of Lucy proceeded smoothly. I called for Lucy, and the cat came dutifully to eat. Michael and I had grabbed the name "Lucy" out of the hat of our favorite baby-boomer television shows. We thought Lucy made perfect sense for an orange female cat who might be as full of mirth as Lucy Ricardo. But I decided that our Lucy needed a more elegant name, one befitting a proper Southern lady whom I would groom and rear as my feline daughter. My nurturing impulses were in their gestational stage.

These feelings were foreign to me. When I attended Wellesley, the competitive environment was particularly hard-driving and relentless. Classroom instruction focused on preparing women to enter the professional workforce, and as such we were advised to be competent and efficient. There seemed to be an unwritten rule that becoming a mother was *verboten*, a waste of our education and feminist indoctrination. What was happening to this Wellesley Girl?

I announced to my parents, siblings, and a few close colleagues at work that Michael and I had adopted a cat, Lucinda Virginia. We could not have been more excited. I also told my cat-loving hairdresser, Joe, about our pet. I knew he would approve because sometimes he became so animated while talking about his own family of cats that I secretly worried he might not trim my bangs evenly. He rightly urged us to bring Lucinda Virginia to his veterinarian's office for an initial exam and checkup. Shortly after the Fourth of July, I made an appointment at the feline-only clinic recommended by Joe. A museum colleague apprised me of the usual trials and tribulations of getting a cat into a carrier. Surely Lucinda Virginia wouldn't mind, I argued.

It took all hands on deck to force the decidedly unladylike, uncharacteristically aggressive cat into the carrier, which I held on my lap in the passenger seat of what Michael and I dubbed our getaway vehicle. Little did he and I know that we not only were taking a five-minute road trip to aid the cat's physical recovery, but that we were due for a life-altering discovery—one that would affect my personal dynamic with the cat.

What's in a Name?

Dr. R. walked into the examining room and efficiently ran through the checklist of standardized questions her clinic had prepared for assessing the condition of a stray cat. She had scribbled "DSH" on her clipboard, and I inquired whether this was a feline acronym. "No, ma'am," she responded with a grin. "DSH means domestic shorthair." Dr. R. asked if the cat had a name. Michael and I smiled and said, "Yes, Lucinda Virginia, and we call her Lucy for short!" The gregarious veterinarian picked up Lucy with one hand, inspected the cat's rear end quickly, and, in the best, straight-out-of-central-casting Southern accent imaginable, said, "Oh, yeaaah. You mean, Mr. Lucy."

Our jaws dropped. Michael and I had not looked closely enough to notice that Lucinda Virginia was a guy. Dr. R. surmised that our "he-cat" had been someone's pet at first and had later been neglected and abused. We asked about the circular red wound, which was healing slowly. She said that she had never seen one that looked exactly like this kind, and that she bet Lucy was not going to tell us what had happened to him. Dr. R. looked Lucy directly in the eyes and asked, "Do you know how lucky you are to have been rescued?" Lucy sat zombielike, staring into space, prompting the veterinarian to caution that our cat seemed "different." "Define different," I demanded. Dr. R. was quick on the draw. "He's spooky." I'll never forget Dr. R.'s additional commentary, and I quote faithfully: "The cat is neurotic, but you can be glad at least that he is not psychotic."

One thing was certain, no matter the official diagnosis of the cat's mental state. Michael and I were not leaving the examining room without renaming Lucy. Lucifer, Luciano, Ludacris, Lucullus, Lucretius... Lucius! Our newly identified son would now be known to the world as Lucius. We also changed Lucius's middle name to that of Lyndon, after Lyndon Baines Johnson (Michael, a diehard Texan, has long admired our nation's thirty-sixth president, a native Texan), making Lucius a triple-L threat.

Lucius felt no pain after his name-changing operation. Lucy morphed into Lucius before our eyes, and Lucius never once looked over his shoulder for another cat when I summoned him by his new name to announce that breakfast or dinner was being served. I also changed Lucius's food, realizing that a strapping young male (Dr. R.'s educated guesstimate: one or two years old) required some hungry-man grub in his daily diet. Plus, Lucius needed to gain weight, though his skinny tail has never caught up with the rest of his body. He wasn't into carbo-loading and started sharing his daily portion of dry food with a young cat who had appeared out of nowhere. The cat had a head the size of a cantaloupe and could not be missed. I wasn't going to use

The Scoop on...

Scooping Cat Litter

I am a sight to behold at the grocery store. Every Saturday, I purchase fifty pounds of non-clumping cat litter, fifty-six cans of wet cat food, and five bags of dry organic cat food. Once, after wheeling my cart with its mountainous haul to the checkout counter, I noticed that the store's manager had stepped in to work the cash register. He seemed intrigued. As he was scanning the items for purchase, he glanced at me and asked, "Got cats?" I was tempted to reply, "No, but I sure love the smell of cat litter."

Cleaning litter boxes at least once a week is a necessity—no ifs, ands, or buts—especially depending on the number of cats in your home. Cats are like humans in this regard: They are appalled by a dirty bathroom. As our cat family expanded, I considered buying self-cleaning, automated litter machines. I fantasized about turning in my latex gloves, discarding the Lysol bottle, and letting the robotic arm take charge of sifting the immediate odor control and long-lasting odor control litters that I mix in each box. But I also heard that cats were disturbed by the noise of the rake scooping and disposing of the litter. So I decided to turn a chore into a more pleasurable routine. If Bobby Flay and other Food Network celebrity chefs can grill, bake, and sauté to background music, then I should be able to scoop competently to the tunes of my choice. I have edited a number of books on modern and contemporary Latin American art, and, as a result, I have grown very fond of bossa nova and samba. I highly recommend these rhythms and beats to accompany your hand moves.

Dr. R.'s lift-and-look method to determine the cat's sex, but I was able to get close enough to make the correct call. "Tom," as we named him, could never be mistaken for a girl.

Lucius and Tom shared their meals on the front and back porches without rancor. Tom wandered often because he was already in tomcat mode, and we were not able to establish a feeding pattern with him until several months later when he began to appear regularly, mostly in need of sustained sustenance but also in need of mating with any available female cat on our street. The slightly tolerable heat of early July became blistering, and Michael and I decided to bring Lucius inside so that he could become a creature of air-conditioned comfort. This time, Michael raised Lucius from the scorching pavement and cradled him like a baby, carrying him ceremoniously through the doorway.

Lucius began to scope our house, sniffing the furniture and carpets as he headed upstairs for further inspections. I worried that he didn't approve of our home decor. When Lucius began to howl, I was puzzled: Was our taste *that* bad? I had majored in art history, for heaven's sake, and I worked for an art museum; I stood by my aesthetic. I wasn't able to read Lucius's mind yet, or to understand the telegraphic look in his eyes and know how to react to it. So I simply picked him up and tried to make conversation with him. "Where did you come from, Lucius? Were you once somebody's kitty?" Lucius's ears perked up at the sound of the word "kitty," causing me to think that he must have been adopted as a kitten. Michael remarked that Lucius looked extremely comfortable in my arms. This was the beginning of a not-so-magnificent obsession on the cat's part, as well as the start of my catering to Lucius's every whim and need.

Michael seconded my appreciation of Lucius. We commented often on the sheer sensation of having another living being in our house. We also took ourselves very seriously as doting parents. We ordered a monogrammed pet cushion for Lucius from L.L. Bean, the first of many purchases that would leave the store's customer service representatives wondering, as our feline family grew, exactly how many children we had brought into this world in a four-year period. We bought virtually every type of cat toy from our neighborhood PetSmart, all to please Lucius. We marveled at how he could jump onto a table set formally for dinner and not disturb a fragile crystal glass. We kissed him on his lips and showered him with praise constantly, just for being Lucius.

We wanted him to trust us and to be at ease. Lucius became frightened on weekends when I removed the broom from the hall closet to tend to housekeeping. Michael and I suspected that someone had hurt him deliberately and repeatedly with a broom handle. Every other day of the week, Lucius followed me around the house in the morning, before I went to work. At night, as soon as I came home, I fell under his watchful gaze.

At the office, some colleagues inquired why I was cutting short a business trip or canceling a plan to attend a conference to pitch the museum's art books. A few others noted that I had not accompanied Michael on his regularly scheduled business trip to Helsinki in August, a trip we had often extended into a vacation. I even didn't travel to visit my parents in Chicago that summer. When confronted with questions about my stay-at-home status, I responded automatically, and sometimes tersely: Lucius. Because of this cat, I was already beginning to see my immediate surroundings differently.

I had been intimidated by the curators—the museum's brain trust—for years. The museum has twelve curatorial departments, and whenever the rest of us, "the have-nots," speak of "the curators," we tend to refer to them in aggregate, as a conglomerate. Although each curator is most definitely an individual, with a strong point of view, the curators en masse have common traits. Their disrespect for my sacrosanct publishing deadlines and their casual put-downs about the over-saturation of a printer's color proofs, among other things, were tiresome, yet I still respected their right to complain. An editor merely could hope to circle their curatorial orbit, never hovering too close to the brilliant, always blazing, celestial bodies, and never critiquing even their roughest drafts too harshly because that would be a breach of unwritten protocol. But at least curators didn't have hairballs.

At home, Lucius's howls and persistent meows were giving me goose bumps. I longed for just a little peace and quiet, some quality time with myself again, and also with Michael. Gone were my easy days of reading a book without a cat repeatedly sprawling on top of it, trying to pry apart dog-eared pages. If Michael and I rented a video, Lucius wanted to sit beside me and watch the film, too. But at least he didn't make ridiculous remarks like "editing could compromise the integrity of my manuscript."

Although the pros of adopting Lucius outweighed the cons, his loyalty became problematic by early September 2000. Lucius adopted an unsettling habit of encircling my feet and making yelping noises, as if he was in heat and I was the object of his desire. This mating-like behavior continued on an on-and-off basis, and I finally placed a call to Dr. R. to convey my concern.

Music to His Ears

"That's an easy one to diagnose," said the wise and delightfully wisecracking veterinarian, again in her pronounced drawl. "He's weird!" Her diagnosis didn't get Lucius off of my leg. And then there was the state of being that I call "interesting weird." I had observed that Lucius seemed especially fond of sacred choral music. I believe it's safe to say that this distinct type of music is an acquired taste among humans, and I had to assume an unusual penchant for a cat. I wondered if, in one of Lucius's previous incarnations, he had been a musician. Perhaps not coincidentally, our historic house was once filled with music and was known to longtime Houstonians for being the site of lively and familial piano recitals. It was only fitting that Lucius would be in tune with the musical heritage of our home.

Just for Lucius, I started listening every Sunday morning to National Public Radio's *With Heart and Voice*. Lucius became familiar with the tranquilizing voice of its host, Richard Gladwell, and with the organ music that opened every program, and he expressed his satisfaction by lying on his back, paws up, enraptured for the full hour (I don't know how to break this news to Lady Gaga, but Lucius Lyndon Lovejoy invented the anthem "Put Your Paws Up!"). I decided to branch out and gauge whether Lucius might share my interest in musicals, and, every Saturday night, he and I listened to some of Broadway's best. I discovered fast that, although Lucius liked the songs, he squirmed when I sang along because I don't have a crystal-clear voice. The lone and notable exception to this rule was when I sang "Moon River" around the house, usually after a screening of *Breakfast at Tiffany's* on Turner Classic Movies and I couldn't get the song out of my head. Lucius liked the refrain, "Wherever you're goin', I'm goin' your way."

Lucius and I grew closer by the day, especially as Michael chased business abroad. Every time Michael left for the airport, he instructed Lucius to protect me, to be the Little Man of the house. Lucius took Michael's counsel to heart—sleeping next to me, placing a paw on my shoulder, and situating his head next to mine on the pillow. Sometimes he even slept on top of my head. I would awaken in the middle of the night to find Lucius staring at me. I kept thinking that if I asked him, "What in the world are you doing?" he would respond, "I am worshipping at the shrine."

Through Lucius, I started to feel intensely connected with all things feline. But our codependency did not come without increasing anxiety on my part. On one hand, I was deeply flattered because anyone who observed us recognized that Lucius loved me dearly. I had read that felines always attach themselves to a "human cat," a replacement for their mother; in the case of male cats, their mothers run them off so that only one male cat comes on the scene and prevails, enabling the reproductive cycle to continue. On the other hand, I worried that Lucius thought that he and I were married. It was time to consult another veterinarian in Dr. R.'s clinic who not only would be frank, but who might be sympathetic to both Lucius's needs and my own cry for help. I was becoming scared of Lucius's dominion over me.

Code Orange: House Call

The new veterinarian made a house call to observe Lucius in his orange-tabby glory, the lord of our crumbling manor. Dr. O. came to us highly recommended, having graduated at the top of her class at Texas A&M University, ranked as among the best veterinary schools in the country. I told Dr. O. that since rescuing Lucius, I had wondered if he was born with a complex. I also confided in her that I was concerned my devotion to Lucius had made him slightly nuts. She observed Lucius hanging around me for nearly two hours and declared that there was a clinical term for his behavior—which she would not modify with "slightly." He had personality disorders and suffered mostly from a fear of abandonment. She also said confidently that he could be treated at her alma mater.

I winced at this last statement for two reasons. First, as we had already learned from taking Lucius to Dr. R.'s office, he suffers from motion sickness. The trip to A&M's campus would take nearly two hours under optimal speeding conditions on the highway from Houston. The second and bigger problem was a thorny issue that I needed to address privately with Michael. He graduated from the McCombs School of Business at the University of Texas at Austin, and the A&M Aggies are the most-hated football rival of the Texas Longhorns. I excused myself to speak with Michael, who lay down the law: "I respect Dr. O.'s authority, but Lucius will not step foot in Aggie territory." Them's fighting words.

Teacher's Pet

I noticed early on that Lucius had an affinity for words. Perhaps in yet another incarnation of this cat's nine lives, he was a lyricist or a novelist. Lucius responds to many more words than the usual number of twenty or so that a cat can master. My pet word in his evolving vocabulary is, not surprisingly, "editor." Lucius has an eye for detail, and he spots a bad manuscript from across a crowded room. One day, before the advent of electronic editing, I was seated at our kitchen counter to begin editing what I suspected—based on the curator's previous performance—was a sloppily written manuscript. I was armed with only one weapon: my red pencil. Lucius kept tapping the sharpened tip of the pencil, playfully suggesting that the manuscript needed a drastic overhaul to improve it. I couldn't get him to stop diverting the pencil from the tall stack of paper, or to refrain from chewing on the pencil's well-worn eraser. But at some point he finally lost interest in the text, a luxury that I can ill afford.

The museum's publishing program is aligned with the institution's mission of bringing art to all people. This philosophy translates to giving every curator

Kitty Con Artists

Let's not fool ourselves. Cats know what we are saying, especially if we are talking about them, and even better if we are praising them. It's a cop-out to say that "treat" is the only word worth repeating to a feline. Cats can recognize a special intonation in one's voice, a mutter under the breath, or a catch in the throat. Much as I think of my cats as my kids, I know that ultimately they cannot vocalize except by way of their meows and sometime shrieks and howls. But they will respond intently and obediently whenever we make time to sit down with them for a cozy chat. Repetition stimulates the curious cat, and I encourage you to converse with your kitty often. You'll be surprised by the number of words and commands that a cat can understand.

an opportunity to be published under the museum's imprint, and that can mean transforming a manuscript from its raw and uncooked form to a grown-up state of flawless fluency. I took this responsibility seriously. What I did not respect were the curators who devalued the privilege afforded by the museum.

No sooner did I take the plunge for a rescue mission of the editorial kind, putting pencil to paper, than Lucius regurgitated his morning meal, soiling the printout and making the text stink in more ways than one. About ten pages in, I came to the sorry conclusion that I, too, could not stomach the text.

For all of Lucius's self-imposed fears and unique eccentricities, not to mention his deserved self-importance, his most special quality is his empathy. This came to light clearly on February 2, 2003, the day that Dinny died. I received the sad news early that morning while at work, and I went home during my lunch break to cry privately. Michael was recuperating from jet lag, brought on by another business trip to Helsinki, and he was prepared to help me work through my grief. What I had not expected was for Lucius to lick the tears falling slowly down my face. I am not so deluded to think that Lucius understood what made me cry—he had never seen me react to pain or anguish. But I am grateful he knew that I needed extra-loving comfort on that day, and that he so willingly obliged.

Don't Let Me Be Misunderstood

With apologies to Michael, I am Lucius's truest soul mate. Whenever I look into Lucius's pea-green eyes, yearning to know what he is thinking, I am reminded of the lyrics to the Animals' hit song (and I know this reference dates me), "Don't Let Me Be Misunderstood": "But I'm just a soul whose intentions are good. Oh, Lord, please don't let me be misunderstood." Lucius suffers from being too smart for his own good. There, I said it.

Sometimes I think of Lucius in editorial terms: If he were a manuscript, how would I edit him? I would be hard-pressed to shape and style him because the parts must stand as they are. The compilation matters most, and only Lucius holds that copyright, enforced in all territories. No degree of animal cloning could capture the depths and nuances of his complex personality—disorder included—and the full majesty of his psychotic being.

Shortly after Michael and I adopted Lucius, I came across a cat cartoon by Leo Cullum in *The New Yorker*. A psychiatrist is counseling a cat with brutal honesty: "You're completely screwed up."

Hmmm. What might make our screwed-up Lucius happy?

Takahashi Hiroaki (Shotei), Japanese, 1871-1945; published by Fusui
Gabo, Japanese, active 1930s, *Cat Prowling Around a Staked Tomato Plant*, 1931

Félix Emile-Jean Vallotton, Swiss, 1865-1925, *Laziness (La Paresse)*, 1896

つれ
づれ

Ishikawa Toraji, Japanese, 1875-1964, *Tsurzure*, from the series *Ten Nudes*, 1934

Toshikata Mizuno, Japanese, 1866-1908, *Woman after a Bath (Married Woman of the Kansei Era)*, from the series *Thirty-six Types of Beauties (Sanjurokkasen)*, 1891-93

p. 37: Utagawa Kunitoshi, Japanese, 1847-1899, *Popular Hotspring Spa for Cats (Ryūkō neko no onse)*, Meiji era

Joseph Wright of Derby, English, 1734-1797, *Dressing the Kitten*, c. 1768-70

Wanda Wulz, Italian, 1903-1984, *Io + Gatto*, 1932

Brassaï, French, born Hungary, 1899-1984, *Cat with Phosphorescent Eyes*, 1936

40

Ron Evans, American, born 1943, *Climbing Cat*, 1983

François Boucher, French, 1703-1770, *La Toilette*, 1742

Brassaï, French, born Hungary, 1899–1984, *Opium Smoker and Cat, Paris*
(Fumeuse d'opium au chat, Paris), c. 1931

Unknown photographer, *Cat posed with Mexican Serape*, c. 1866-68

G.T., possibly English, *Portrait of a Woman*, c. 1830

Marcus Stone, English, 1840-1921, *Il y en a toujours un autre*, 1852

46

Yamamoto Masao, Japanese, born 1957, *Untitled*, from the series *A Box of Ku*, 2001

Yva (Else Neuländer-Simon), German, 1900-1942, *Untitled*, c. 1931

Chapter 3

Smitten

Lydia

I was perfectly content having Lucius as our only cat-child, albeit a challenging one at that. Still, Michael and I talked openly—surely Lucius could not understand every word in our conversation— about finding another feline, not only a companion for Lucius, but for us, as well. I was in awe of people who methodically timed the births of their children, as best as they could, so as not to deal with two toddlers in diapers and eventually pay two college tuitions simultaneously. Now we were mapping a new landscape, exclusively with cats, and there was something to be said for family planning.

When Michael and I made up our minds to adopt a playmate for Lucius, we were advised by Dr. O. to adopt a female kitten. The consensus was that Lucius would not feel threatened by a youthful cat of the opposite sex, and he would welcome such a newcomer to the family. Michael and I deliberated and discussed the kind of cat we wanted, and we decided that a grey tabby would be visually compatible with an orange tabby and would like living in our house of subdued colors and antique faded carpets.

As had become our new custom every weekend, Michael and I ventured to our neighborhood PetSmart. One Sunday in late September, a Houston-based animal welfare group named H.O.P.E. (Homeless and Orphaned Pets Endeavor) set up a mini-adoption center near the cat-food and cat-merchandise aisles at the store. The cat carriers in the adoption area were stacked floor to ceiling, like a tic-tac-toe grid. At the bottom of the stack, I glimpsed an undersized grey kitten crouched in the rear corner of a carrier, which the kitten shared with much larger cats. I thought to myself, "This kitten is doing nothing to get noticed and is doing everything to get left behind." But I had noticed the kitten because of her tiny size, and especially because my sight line is considerably lower than that of the average-sized person. According to a sign hung outside of the carrier, the little grey kitten with the disproportionately large ears and the mesmerizing gooseberry eyes was a four-month-old named Kirstie. I instructed Michael to take a look at her while I pursued my usual pathways through PetSmart, searching for victuals and presents with which to spoil Lucius.

I returned to the adoption site to find the kitten crawling back and forth on Michael's broad shoulders. He said approvingly, "She's a good kitty." We read the description of the six-pound Kirstie: She had been rescued from a Siamese cattery in Dallas, where she was living in squalid conditions, specifically in a concrete-floored room with as many as thirty other cats. When I read the paperwork on Kirstie, I had a funny feeling that her breeders must have been experimenting freely, creating their own feline version of Frankenstein: Kirstie was half-Siamese and half-wildcat, part Egyptian Mau and part grey tabby.

She had spots running up and down her board-flat stomach, and this fashion-forward pattern added to her exotic qualities.

My first thought was that Lucius would be thrilled to have such a fascinating creature scampering around our house. My second thought was that we couldn't do "this" to Lucius. He would become angry and upset. He would never forgive us for invading his turf, and I had to speak up for him. "Tough," said Michael, rather gruffly. "She's coming home with us."

We completed the adoption papers and passed the H.O.P.E. test of parental approval with flying colors, probably because the adoption agents perceived from our profuse and verbose descriptions of Lucius (we desperately needed an on-site editor) that we were kind of crazy about our one cat at home (you think?) and most likely would become even crazier about having two cats. The agents guided Kirstie into a pet carrier, and while Michael and I walked to our car, we renamed her. This time there was not a compelling biological reason to come up quickly with a new name for our new cat. Our wish was simple: We wanted to make this kitten ours, and we decided on the name of Lydia Benson, in memory of Michael's great-great-grandmother.

Lydia cried at the top of her lungs, wailing during the car ride home. Again, I thought I heard the not-so-subtle voice of Lucius imploring me, "Don't bring another cat into *my* house."

Et tu, Lucius?

Lucius was sitting regally on the velvet couch in the den. He looked satisfied, even smug, until he sensed that another cat had entered the all-Lucius zone. I had no idea about how to properly introduce a new cat into a household ruled by a resident cat. I opened the carrier door wide, directly in front of Lucius, and let Lydia loose. I was prepared to take my lead from him.

The how-do-you-do session was a hissing disaster. Lucius had a look of absolute betrayal and glared at me. He chased Lydia around the first floor of our house; fortunately, she had the presence of mind to hide underneath a bolster on the same velvet couch that Lucius had appropriated earlier for his throne. Because of Lydia's size, I was concerned for her safety. I moved fast to scoop Lydia up and whisk her away to a place where Lucius could not find her. Off we went to the garage apartment at the back of the house.

Lydia demonstrated her creativity by making a little nest for herself in the apartment, which Michael quickly rearranged to suit the frenetic habits of a youthful kitten. He built a makeshift jungle gym by reconfiguring an unmatched set of chairs stored in the apartment, and I furtively hijacked some of Lucius's toys for her to play with while she was forced to live alone. In the first few days after adopting Lydia, Michael visited her while she was sequestered, whereas I focused on trying to keep Lucius cheerful. I skimmed a book on how to successfully integrate new cats into a household, and I brought Lydia to our house each night for the equivalent of a papal visitation with Lucius. He agreed to give her an audience but treated Lydia like his personal cat toy, swatting her for the heck of it. And yet... as the Beatles once sang, there was "something in the way" that Lucius looked at Lydia that made me think he would like her.

About two weeks into the scheduled visitations, I realized that Lucius had fooled me. He was pining for Lydia. I spied on him peering out of the French doors in the den and looking up at the windows of the apartment. Lydia positioned herself in the window closest to our house so that Lucius could see her clearly, playing Juliet to his Romeo. If Lucius could have bayed at the moon to announce his newfound desire of wanting/needing Lydia, he would have done so.

Before the month ended, I rescued Lydia from solitary confinement and brought her inside our house. I considered not going to work on that day because of fear of leaving her and Lucius without a chaperone. Would he have a "good day"? But I had underestimated Lydia. She relied on one of the oldest tricks in the book of female sorcery, flirtation, and had introduced Lucius to the land of sweet licks and other forms of mutual grooming. When I returned home, I was ecstatic to find the happy couple snuggling on an antique twin-size brass bed in the guest bedroom upstairs that I also use as my home office. There could be no doubt: Lucius was smitten with Lydia.

Lydia loved the coziness of our home so much, and now loved her Lucius so much, that any sign of upheaval unnerved her. Shortly after we adopted her, Lydia exhibited some signs of a mild stomach ache, and her lethargy worried me. I wanted to take her to the veterinarian's office, but the sound of the carrier door opening (cat's interpretation: leaving my home by force) sent her fleeing to a safe spot under our bed. I was moved by her fear: She must have thought she was going to be an orphan again, that we were returning her to the cattery because she was not feeling like her usual self, and she must have thought, too, she was being punished. After many failed attempts at retrieving her from under the bed, I phoned Dr. O. and requested a house call.

As soon as I opened the front door to greet Dr. O., our phony patient sprang to life, eager to introduce a new game that showcased her budding imagination. Lydia the Matador grasped a feathered wand in her mouth, calculated the distance between where she was standing with the wand and the "bull" (a stationary chair), and then ran the distance as fast as she could. I had just read an article praising cats for their ingenuity and ability to integrate suitable elements in their home with their behavioral instincts, and here was living proof. Dr. O. proclaimed that Lydia was the most focused and impressive kitty she had encountered in a long time. Lucius looked on appreciatively, and Michael and I congratulated each other on having such a smart kitty. I also was struck by the realization that Lydia was the closest I could get to claiming I had a daughter.

A League of Her Own

If Michael and I had become the parents of a girl, we would have encouraged her to take part in certain Southern traditions. Shortly after I relocated from Chicago to Houston, I was accepted into the Junior League. I joined the league because I had a genuine desire to serve the Houston-area community as a trained volunteer, and I wanted to meet like-minded women. Giving up my base in Chicago meant losing regular touch with my girlfriends there, and the league had a built-in population from which I could draw and make new friends.

The league was in transition in the early 1990s, attracting increasingly large numbers of women who work full-time. Although, to a certain extent, the negative stereotype of the league as a bastion of conservatism and social exclusivity prevails, the Houston organization's clout of disbursing more than $2 million annually in volunteer time and direct financial support speaks volumes. The Houston league also has a long-standing record of service at the Museum of Fine Arts, where league members give docent tours to teachers and schoolchildren year-round. For me, becoming a Junior Leaguer was a win–win scenario.

The Houston league's headquarters building might be called a cross between Tara from *Gone with the Wind* and an English country house. Because of the enormity of the physical complex, volunteers are in demand at all hours to staff the various functions held there. My most gratifying placement involved marketing the league's first two award-winning cookbooks. I got Michael involved behind the scenes, and we planned menus for every social and family event that a member might host—from September tailgating parties to June graduation luncheons. Our home-grown menus were published in the league's monthly magazine and newsletter and printed on "seat sheets" distributed at the league's monthly meetings. Talk about targeted marketing: League members could not take their seats without picking up the menus placed on every chair in the house. Eventually, Michael and I adapted our popular surf 'n turf menu for the cats' delectation.

While chatting with other Sustaining members (translation: women over 40) in the league's kitchen one day, I overheard a volunteer discussing the merits of "Take Your Daughter to Work Day." I wasn't embarrassed by my budding

The Scoop on...

Staying as Young as a Kitten and Avoiding Zombie Status

Having children late in life is a special challenge, so I have been told. Keeping up with a kitten is a sport probably best left for the young, although even as I grow older I cannot imagine saying I will never adopt another newborn or months-old cat again. I have lost a lot of sleep from young cats climbing on me, sleeping on top of me, leaping over me, and licking me. I also have devoted substantial time to chasing after youthful cats with very healthy appetites, trying to coax them to eat more slowly and to savor their hearty meals. Would I trade those hectic and sometimes zany moments for boredom? Of course not! If you are planning to adopt a kitten, be prepared to be on call at all times during that first impressionable year. Kittens like to test boundaries, and you need to establish yours up front. For instance, if you don't want a sleeping companion in the form of a cat, then shut the door to your bedroom from the get-go. That advice is easy for me to dispense now, many years after ushering eight kittens into adulthood and arriving at my office resembling the so-called walking dead.

maternal feelings for Lydia. I simply didn't know then how to introduce her into a conversation about parenting. While league members were carpooling with their daughters to dance classes, I was left behind driving Lydia to only one place outside of our home: a veterinary office. I couldn't compare notes in the same way, yet I never gave fellow league members a chance to understand the dynamic of my family life at home.

On the surface, what was not to like about Lydia? Southern women like steel magnolias, and Lydia had lots of potential. But I didn't know what to make of Lydia in her early years—a mysterious creature who could not shed the unmistakable body odor she had acquired from living with so many other cats in deplorable surroundings. She was rough around the edges. I couldn't make her fit the traditional definition of femininity that was still ingrained in me, the one that insists on a woman wearing lipstick whenever she heads to PetSmart. I should have been proud that Lydia was in a league of her own.

Lydia slurped and dug her claws into upholstery with a vengeance. She drank water clumsily from the kitchen faucet and demanded that I rub her petite derrière in a robust fashion. Round and round went my fingers as I recited Lydia's favorite phrase that Michael had so crudely coined: "butt scratchin'." Watching Lydia steal toilet paper and prance up and down the stairs with reams of it streaming from her chin also was not one for the record book on womanliness. She reserved her best behavior for a plumber, though.

I was preparing for a dinner party when the kitchen garbage disposal died a sudden death. I paged a local repair service, and a plumber arrived to save the evening. He deposited his oversized toolbox on the floor, where he would have immediate access to all of the various replacement parts—an unwitting tactical mistake. Lydia saw that the contents of the toolbox were easily in reach, and she sprung into action, grabbing several small mechanical pieces by her teeth and front paws and hiding them upstairs. Who could have predicted that my darling wisp of a girl essentially had the balls to take on a plumber five times her size, sending him on a wild chase through the house? I felt like a hostage negotiator persuading her to release the stolen goods.

With each week, Lydia was turning into a diva (a smelly one at that), vocalizing a mile a minute—befitting her half-Siamese ancestry—and dishing out orders in the process. I now know that, unless there is "a Lucius" at home, a female cat unequivocally rules the house; in my early days of becoming Cat Lady, I simply assumed Lydia was prissy and bossy. Here's to the authentic skinny bitch.

Just like any couple, Lucius and Lydia started having issues, feuding over food, property, and territory. I advised Michael to take note, and cynically suggested that we commission a smiling portrait from one of my artist-friends: This was our new nuclear family.

Lydia Bin Laden

I began to wonder if Lydia would ever slow down. Her high-powered metabolism was fueled by a fussy appetite and a rigid diet. She could leap tall kitchen cabinets in a single bound, and she could run through the house with the speed of an Olympic athlete. Not knowing then that a cat's one-year birthday indicates the beginning of a slowing-down process, I could only dream of when Lydia would not awaken me at 3:00 a.m., applying her warm and bristly tongue to my face, commanding me to open a can of cat food three hours ahead of the official feeding schedule, or to turn on a faucet so that she could drink running water, or to scratch her fanny rigorously. I still laugh over one embarrassing episode with Lydia, from which I suspect my museum colleague never recovered.

I had returned from a business trip to Mexico City to plan a book on Latin American colonial art. After resuming my work and home routines, Michael and I invited my colleague for cocktails so that we could rehash the two-day editorial meetings. Mr. Warren, a decorative arts expert, is also known for his impeccable manners. Our guest took his place in a Mission rocker, and no sooner had he raised his glass in a toast to Mexico and the arts than Lydia leaped on top of the back of the rocker in a stealth attack. She started swinging to and fro, trilling and cooing and leaning over his shoulder, as if she longed to chat with him about silver tea services and blue-and-white ceramics. Mr. Warren promptly christened her Lydia Bin Laden.

In all fairness, Lydia is not a terrorist. When I fantasize about what she would be like if she were my flesh-and-blood daughter, my mind wanders in several directions: the opera singer with the beautiful lilting voice, the plumber with the quick dexterity for fixing broken parts, and the girly girl who would enjoy an all-expense-paid shopping spree for cosmetics at Sephora (lots of eyeliner and mascara to accentuate her Nefertiti-esque eyes).

So there we were, the four of us, Michael and I and Lucius and Lydia. My husband (Michael, not Lucius) and I had found domestic bliss in the form of two cats who themselves had made a pact to become partners for life. We were a manageable family unit, and our decision to adopt two cats still fell within the confines of social acceptability.

If timing is everything, as it is especially in publishing, then the planets were aligned one morning in late October, still in the first year of the new millennium. Something was in the air, and the bubble containing a semblance of normality burst. The world around me was about to experience a *cat*alytic change.

Outside the Box

Cat Lady Camouflage

I have no need to go undercover as Cat Lady. On the contrary; I'm excited about a new business proposition. Wouldn't it be great if the aestheticians at Lancôme or Clinique would create a cosmetic concealer specifically for camouflaging a Cat Lady's markings? I try to apply my under-eye concealer (a cut above the kind that gives a glow-in-the-dark, raccoon-like effect) to cover the affectionate scratches I get from our cats. I also use a secondary concealer that is supposed to take the red out of mosquito bites. All of this is to no avail.

Perhaps I can convince Dr. O. to market "Veterinarian's Formula" concealer. In response to cats demonstrating their love intensely, Dr. O. can cater to the Cat Ladies of the world who long only to wear their hearts on their sleeves, and to hide their kitties' scratches.

Chapter 4

Ensnared

Lillie

*W*hen I first saw Lillie Delilah Lovejoy, it was impossible to comprehend then what is so clear to me now. My future life as Cat Lady would begin to come into focus with the arrival of this tiny calico kitty on our back deck—the designated landing spot for so many of the abandoned cats whom I would rescue. Lillie would teach me that the central theme of my personal story is that nothing would fall into place perfectly. I would not be equipped to predict a plot at Catland, I would not be able to point exactly to an "I-can-see-it-coming" dramatic arc. I would not be inclined to swear on the outcome or to guarantee a happy ending.

Unlike my line of work, where I am paid to forecast and to connect A to B to C—and always with the expectation that I must deliver an on-time and salable product—I had no idea where I was going in my newly parallel universe consisting of felines. Maybe that lack of certainty was okay. For an artist, it's cool, even hip, to be defiantly uncertain about where the hand and the paintbrush may lead, and the results are often spectacular.

I knew enough as an editor to understand that I was approaching that moment in a classic story that is familiarly termed "Crossing the Threshold." Only this was not the common "boy meets girl" tale. This was "lady meets cats." The fact that I was so uncharacteristically willing to enter uncharted territory was a revelation to me. All I could do was follow Lillie's paws and listen to my heart beat.

Lillie looked to be only about six months old, and she already knew how to make an entrance. I wondered if such a drop-dead-gorgeous creature could be the feline incarnation of Angelina Jolie. Like the ravishing Ms. Jolie, this vivacious cat had movie-star charisma. She also radiated sensuality and sexuality.

When Lillie breathed, I heard sighs. All I had to do was ask those big-headed, jowly-cheeked tomcats who paced up and down our driveway and circled our backyard gate aggressively, longing for a closer look at Lillie and angling for a fighting chance with her. It is no wonder that I entertained so quickly the thought of toppling our peaceful cart of two cats at home by adding another feline. In the art world, the lure of an exquisite object transcends its physicality. Lillie's appeal was equally mesmerizing.

Mergers and Acquisitions

Usually, I think of acquisitions in terms of commodities. Through my previous employment at Sotheby's, I had been given a front-row seat to the performance of art auction-goers who are constantly on the lookout, bidding on notable acquisitions at sometimes astronomical costs. I was familiar as well with a different sort of bounty hunter, the big-league art collector, who foregoes the wild ride of the auction and instead goes the distance around the globe, adding unrivaled treasures to his or her trove.

Acquiring art is known to be an ordained and legal form of addiction, with the excitement of the chase followed by the fulfillment of seizing the grand prize. I have been in close contact with such thrill-seekers during all of my days in the art world, and some people are consumed more by greed than by passion for art itself. I, too, will admit to a lust for acquiring artworks and objects, though my acquisitions register more along the fault lines of shabby chic compared with museum-caliber holdings.

Long before cats dominated, or, more accurately, controlled our lives, Michael and I went antiquing every weekend. We had owned our historic home, in one of Houston's officially sanctioned historic neighborhoods, for only a few years, and we had dived into learning about the corresponding decorative arts and furnishings of the Arts and Crafts period. Michael and I enjoyed pawing through garage and estate sales and resale shops for buried treasure. We often returned home victorious, quickly building a modest collection of American art pottery that we fondly termed the "Cracked Pot Collection." Michael and I bought the pottery out of a love for the varied colors and matte or mottled surfaces, and for the creative spirit in which the bowls and vases were made. None of the objects was in perfect condition or qualified for profitable resale, and we reasoned that we were the cracked pots who were turned on by shards of art. Perhaps the broken pottery sitting on junkshop shelves was lying in wait for a reason: Could I recognize its potential to be artfully arranged?

So it is true that I understood the warm and inherently selfish feelings that are associated with ownership, and I also was aware that the feeding frenzy can assume a life of its own. But my hobby was confined to acquiring antique collectibles—inanimate objects that are shuffled, re-hung, or stored as part of a carefully planned rotation—while my profession was focused on fabricating art books that are filed on shelves for reading and periodic consultation, or displayed on coffee tables to make a sophisticated impression. To think seriously about acquiring another cat, the irresistible Lillie, necessitated being open to unimagined possibilities. This vibrant creature would require sustained care and attention.

Although the delicacy of Lillie's face reminded me of that of a nineteenth-century French or German antique doll, Lillie was not made of porcelain. She also was not tame, as demonstrated whenever I attempted to pet her on one of her guest appearances in the backyard. Nonetheless, I could not help but be enamored of Lillie, and I was not going to give up on her. I was ensnared.

The Scoop on...

Faking Atmosphere for Your Cat

Dr. O. once told me that, if I could ask a cat about a lifestyle preference, the cat would vote for outdoors, paws down. Keeping cats outdoors is probably much easier for many people than bringing them indoors. A cat living outside can take care of personal business, so to speak, and there will not be any traces left behind. To me, the worries about the cat's safety—encountering vicious animals, dodging speeding traffic, and so forth—outweigh the perks of foregoing litter-box duty. Keep in mind these two words: "Build vertical." Re-create the excitement of the outdoors by setting up vertical spaces for exploration. Weather permitting, open your windows and let the scent of the outdoors fill your home. There is nothing wrong with faking atmosphere for your cat: Buy some $1.99 "cat grass" at PetSmart, put the container on your kitchen counter, and watch your cat dive in. Felines know that the grass can be greener indoors.

A Sucker for Beauty

Lillie must have sensed that I was a sucker for beauty, or maybe she knew somehow that formal and theoretical discussions of beauty were once part of my background as a student of art history. In any event, she was strutting her stuff, working it, doing the catwalk on an imaginary runway that, in real life, was the back deck of our house. Lillie had caught on that Michael and I could see her from the French doors in the den, where we regrouped after work to watch the nightly news. Whenever Michael saw Lillie, he commented, "On a scale of 10, with 10 being the most beautiful, that cat is off the charts."

I kept thinking that Lillie looked like another cat I had seen. In the checkout lane at PetSmart, I noticed a cover of *Cat Fancy* magazine featuring a photograph of a Norwegian Forest Cat. Paging through the cover story, I made a mental note that Lillie bore a remarkable resemblance to the Norwegian breed, what with the elaborate furry ruff around her neck and her communicative green eyes. Before too long, though, I was struck by the more accurate realization that Lillie reminded me of a cat whom only a master photographer could have conjured.

From an art book that I had edited in the mid-1990s, I recalled that Brassaï had brilliantly turned his camera lens on cats who frequented the streets and alleyways of Paris, or who perched decoratively in the windowsills of Parisian ateliers and apartments. The French doors at our home may have lacked charming French lace curtains to adorn them, but, to me, Lillie unquestionably was worthy of Brassaï's unerring eye for beauty. In my mind, I whisked Lillie away to the City of Light, where she could have joined other notable felines that had served as artists' muses. Lillie would have liked the attention that comes from being a handpicked model.

The more occasions that I had to observe Lillie, the more I respected that she was too proud to beg for food. She would not even stoop to conquer. Her method of capturing my fancy—which meant toying with my heart—was to raise her bushy plumed tail and twirl it around like Beyoncé performing with a boa. These efforts to claim my attention were redundant because Lillie could not be expected to grasp what I had already concluded: I was destined to do as she pleased. Michael and I wanted to acquire Lillie for all of the right reasons, which meant we wanted to adopt her for life.

There is no need for me to provide further details that anthropomorphize Lillie. She has human qualities, evidenced especially when she turns the heads of men—my husband; my other husband, Lucius; and the chorus of neighborhood tomcats. Lucius acted silly when he saw Lillie sidling up to the French doors. Surprisingly, he wasn't upset about her encroaching on his sacred ground, as had been the case initially with the arrival of Lydia. Instead, Lucius aimed to look both nonplussed and cavalier as he approached the doors to appraise the fetching Lillie. Perhaps she exuded some sort of come-hither scent that has yet to be bottled and patented for feline use. He also tried to muffle his heavy panting. Lucius knew Lydia was observing him from close range whenever he gave Lillie a head-to-toe onceover.

The Heat Is On

I observed feline female jealousy for the first time with Lydia and Lillie. I was accustomed to female competition at Wellesley, both over academics—"have you finished your honor's thesis yet?"—and over intramural tennis—"did you beat your opponent?"—and I had encountered female rivalries throughout my career and even in my volunteer capacity at the Junior League. I was familiar with the unbecoming term "hissy fit," and now I had a better sense of the origin of its meaning. As Lydia stared forlornly at Lucius, silently entreating him to pay attention to her exclusively, Lillie responded by turning up the heat. I knew that a well-balanced life was too short for hissy fits, and I was grateful for the impenetrable glass doors that separated the two female cats. Lydia did not want any competition, but Michael and I needed Lillie to stay in close proximity. We believed that familiarity would breed trust and that we could coax Lillie to come live with us at Catland.

Although Lillie was so young, she was wise beyond her years in her ability to get her message across. My colleagues often flatter me by commenting that I listen to people without turning the conversation around and making it about me. This is a gift I inherited from my mother. We Southerners like to gab, to converse, and I truly enjoy hearing others' stories. For whatever reason, people feel comfortable telling me personal, often intimate, details of their lives.

In a different, but complementary, fashion, I was able to heed Lillie's silent calls for help. Whenever we saw Lillie pressing her nose to the glass, we responded by giving her food and water. The challenge in trying first to tame Lillie was that she was elusive. Channeling a *femme fatale*, she seemed to relish playing hard to get. Lillie thrived on freedom, and we guessed that she had never experienced confinement. She also had marked our house as a reliable stopping point on her nightly perambulations, a place where she could count on getting a square meal. Lillie wanted to be a part of our lives, at least from the mercenary standpoint of regular feedings, but she wanted to call the shots.

Prior to meeting Lillie, I had never encountered the term "feral." When I called the veterinarian's office to discuss Lillie, I mistook the vet tech's Texas accent for "Fair Isle" cat, and I didn't understand how a cat could resemble a sweater from J. Crew or a similar purveyor of preppy clothing. I learned that Lillie fit the definition of a feral cat, described as "a cat born outside and who [I changed the word from "that"] has never lived with a human family, or a house cat who [ditto] strayed from home and over time has thrown off the effects of domestication and reverted to a wild state." Lillie wasn't wild, just wildly sexy.

As I was discovering my new calling for taking care of cats, I heard the characteristic calling of a cat in heat. This mating song and dance continued for several weeks, and soon I noticed that Lillie had gained weight. She always maintained a dainty figure, even though she ate heartily. Despite not having been pregnant, I have a weird knack for recognizing others' states of maternity well before the tell-tale signs. I also have a fascination with twins, satisfied by the births of my brother's identical twin sons and my brother-in-law's fraternal twins. I had a strong suspicion—supported by Lillie's multiple

Out, Damned Cat Treat

I could kick myself for introducing our ten cats to the world of treats. Am I an enabler, someone who has turned cats into junkies? Our cats are always waiting by the back door when I return from the grocery store, at the ready to inspect the contents of the bags I've brought home. It seems that I can never buy enough treats.

As I was tossing an empty bag of treats into the recycling bin one day, I noticed that the bag had a new look. I don't know why I bothered to study the label of something about to be discarded, but I laughed when I read the following lines: "Home. The vast inner kingdom. Within these four walls of comfort and quiet, I am the hunter." Is the copywriter thinking that a Cat Lady will read this purple prose aloud to her cats? Or does the treat manufacturer have evidence that cats can read for themselves? I've never asked them, but I sincerely hope that our cats do not endorse sentence fragments.

audibles—that Lillie was "with child" (as my Southern grandmother used to say with embarrassment about a pregnant woman), and that she was probably expecting more than one.

I became obsessed thinking about Lillie's impending motherhood and also about the practicality of caring for a pregnant animal. Even very diminutive cats such as Lillie can produce a litter numbering five or more kittens. Lillie was a child herself; how could she be mature enough to take care of her own children? I announced my prognostication to Michael, who was not in the mood to think about the ramifications of expanding our two-cat family. He thought I was becoming so caught up in "catdom" that I could no longer see straight. But I was convinced of my instincts and resolved to monitor the situation.

Call and Response

Michael and I became frantic, fearing the worst, when Lillie disappeared. Our intent to rescue Lillie was based on an unqualified desire to bring her inside. She was too small to live a life on the streets without injury. I wondered if her survivor's luck had worn out.

Michael was traveling on international business to Germany, which left me to my own devices of trying to locate Lillie. I called for her while cruising up and down the neighborhood streets—minus a squad car—though probably resembling an agitated person handcuffed inside of one. When Michael returned, I broke the news that it appeared Lillie was not to be found.

As was his habit after an overseas trip requiring a major leap in time zones, Michael was exhausted and jet-lagged. He had been home only a few days, and by the weekend he was still struggling to regain his equilibrium. I clearly recall the Sunday morning in early December after his return, when Michael abandoned all hope of restfulness and awakened about 4:00 a.m. I heard him shuffling papers and brewing coffee in the kitchen, and I, too, gave up on sound sleep. I figured we might as well start our day early and feed our two cats, devoting the requisite time to worshipping Lucius. I headed downstairs.

I was convinced that I heard kittens meowing as they were making their way from underneath the deck of our house onto the cobblestone pavement in our backyard. My curiosity was such that, even in a slight state of undress, I went outside to investigate further. When I found an adorable grey tabby and two precious calicos, I couldn't restrain myself. I ran toward them excitedly, and out of the corner of my eye I saw that Lillie had arrived. She looked sheepish, but she was also beaming about being a new parent.

Woo-hoo, over the threshold I go!

Perkins

T. J.

Miss Tommie

Trapped

Who's Your Daddy?

I found myself asking the three kitties that probing question on our first day of getting acquainted with each other. I already harbored strong suspicions, given that one tomcat stood out in the crowd of Lillie's suitors, but I had to ask. Then I realized that there was no need to inquire because the answer was staring me in the face, provided by the innocent-looking visage of the classic grey tabby. Like father, like son: Just as Pablo Picasso's male offspring could not have been mistaken for any other, so, too, was the tabby kitten the absolute spitting image of another famously macho guy, Tom. He was the one male cat who walked with a swagger up and down the sidewalks in our neighborhood, and he took no prisoners. The two calicos were mirror twins and resembled Lillie, although neither at such a tender age held a candle to her beauty. All three kitties had unusually big, mitten-like paws for their diminutive size, just as was the case with their mother, and their tails gave every indication that they would grow to become bushy and fluffy with age.

By default, Michael and I had earned naming rights as the unplanned adoptive parents of Lillie's children. We jumped on the name T.J. for Tom Junior, and decided on Perkins Aurelia (after one of Michael's aunts) for one of the calicos, and Thomasina Dinny (after the incomparable Dinny) for the other. As avid cat lovers, we had won the daily double, hitting the jackpot by increasing our feline family from three to six overnight. But we felt numbed by the instant responsibility of caring for this many so soon. It was one thing to be reasonably adept at multitasking at the office, going back and forth between curators and graphic designers and printers. But the elective parenting of six cats would present a different set of real-world, as opposed to art- and book-world, challenges. Had it been only a matter of months since I had shaken up my previously systematic, predictably linear world?

Like all editors, I am accustomed to eliminating redundancies, stripping excessive adjectives from nouns and verbs, paring thoughts, and tightening syntaxes. The other doctor who was a major influence on my life, Peter Marzio (a Ph.D., never a veterinarian), was not only my boss, but, more importantly, the museum's director, and he was fond of saying "KISS" (Keep It Simple, Stupid) whenever he read a cluttered and jargon-laden manuscript. Dr. Marzio taught me how to KISS, and I bow to his theory of economy. Editors do not accumulate excess verbiage by nature, yet there I was at home, adding, not subtracting, and expanding, instead of contracting, our family of cats. I needed to clarify the unclear, just as I would in dissecting a manuscript, and to reflect on this sudden attraction to wanting and having more. What was I after: the presumed happiness of the cats, or my own? Or would I define happiness as an entangled combination of the two?

While contemplating my state of adoptive motherhood, and how I could remain faithful to core editorial principles and values, I was also thinking about Tom, who was not winning any points as an absentee dad. But the ever-luminous Lillie was present. I focused on her intently as she adapted to her new role of parenting T.J., Perkins, and Thomasina. I had imagined that, like many beautiful, self-absorbed, and vain women, Lillie would not carve out ample time to look out for the needs of others. It turns out that I was wrong in this harsh assessment, for Lillie took to motherhood naturally, and she inspired me to feel even more protective toward her and all of our cats.

I loved to watch Lillie groom T.J., Perkins, and Thomasina, whom I nicknamed "Miss Tommie." Lillie caressed the three kittens gently, and even when she grabbed each one by the neck, moving them from a part of the backyard to another to seek shade, she did so gingerly and as if she had read a manual on responsible parenting. I had not taken over these duties for Lillie yet.

Michael and I still had not tamed or domesticated Lillie, and we needed to reinforce our message to her that home meant safety, that wandering the streets could take its toll on her. Once, when she crossed the busy street in front of our house, successfully darting several speeding cars in her path, Michael started waving his hands frenetically and shouted, "Lillie, come home." And we sensed that, finally, she fundamentally understood that our home had become her home.

Animal Kingdom

Home for Lillie and her three kittens necessitated our creating a weather-proofed backyard. Although Michael and I had never gone camping together, or canoed or hiked as a couple, we found ample reasons to consult sales catalogues promoting the great outdoors. We sought to create what in the art world is termed an "immersive environment." Michael purchased oversized umbrellas under which we could serve the cats their fresh food and water during inclement weather; I ordered plush, water-repellant doormats on which they could recline; and the like. We bought electric-heating pads that warmed rapidly to the touch of a cat's body. With pleasure, Michael and I went overboard in our efforts to ensure the comfort of Lillie and her children. We developed a handy system that we thought was foolproof on a 24/7 basis: four bowls of water and four bowls of dry food for four outdoor cats. This gesture of magnanimity toward Lillie *et al.* proved to be our downfall when our backyard became a way station for other animals from unknown walks of life.

Tom, aka Daddy, appeared daily, wanting a piece of the gravy train. If he didn't show up, we assumed he was on a mating binge. To see Tom, his progeny, and Lillie at the same place at the same time meant taking in a broad swath of cats. Counting Tom, there were five felines sleeping in and feeding from our backyard. We were well on the "who-would-have-thunk-it?" road to creating our own adaptation of *Animal Kingdom*.

Meanwhile, Lucius and Lydia were taking keen notice of the incessant scurrying of cats in the backyard and their playful chasing on the deck. Lucius had a bemused look on his face that seemed to say, "You have got to be kidding me." He did not believe in strength in numbers. Lucius swooned every time he saw Lillie, and Lydia continued to be jealous over his attraction to Lillie. But the outdoor cats kept to their business and never challenged the indoor cats. The only complication arose when Michael resumed a hectic international travel schedule. Much as I like to think of myself as an independent woman, I thought I needed Michael's hands to help keep the assembly line in motion. I fell back on my safety net, a checklist, and seeing the daily requirements on paper made me confident that I could master singlehandedly the newest set of challenges.

What I wasn't prepared for was encountering other denizens of the neighborhood that had learned of the free-meals-a-day program at our house. The constant supply of food in our backyard soon attracted families of raccoons and possums. Early one morning, I glanced out the back door to check whether Lillie and her children had already arrived for their breakfast. I screamed when I saw an adult raccoon eating the cats' leftover food from the previous evening. Michael was home and ran to my rescue, relieved to know that "it was only a raccoon," as he put it dismissively, and not a burglar attempting to break in.

"Hey, look at those whoppers," added Michael, pointing to two beefy possums peering from a low branch of the pecan tree that dominates our backyard. Michael's makeshift solution for warding off the wildlife was to breathe heavily into a rusty musical instrument he had saved from childhood and that had not improved with age. The dismal sound sent the wildlife scattering, and they returned only occasionally, when the spirit moved them. I was beginning to envision another *Grey Gardens* in our midst.

Even though Lillie was surrounded by many other animals, both her own kin and nonrelatives, she stood out in a crowd. Watching her reminded me of what I thought to be her human counterpart, a Southern belle holding court at a debutante ball. I kept a close eye on Lillie because she was already past the recommended age for spaying, and we needed to trap her for this procedure. We also needed to be responsible for her children, once they reached an age when spaying and neutering became essential.

A Family Affair

All of this was dizzying to Michael and me, and I wasn't able to learn quickly enough to help reset ourselves. While I was studiously reading up on the reproductive cycles of female cats, Lillie was succumbing to her hormonal urges. Tom was lurking, awaiting Lillie's signals. I heard her long and high-pitched moans one night, and I wished I could have had a candid mother–daughter talk: "Think twice about what you're doing, young lady, and you better not get pregnant again."

My worrying about Lillie did nothing to quench her insatiable desire to mate with Tom. It was not possible for another male cat to advance with Lillie, period. Tom was too formidable a force, and even the raccoons and possums ran when they saw him arrive at the food trough. Though Tom was young, the wise-guy look on his face reminded me of a crusty old sailor's. Tom alone was willing to stand guard in our backyard and monitor Lillie's siren call.

I also began to wonder if Lillie and Tom could be related because of their body language. They seemed sympathetic to each other, as if they shared a special connection, more so than what might be expected of a tomcat circling a female cat in heat, brought together not only by biological impulses but also by the vital need for fresh food and clean water. This possibility of a blood relationship intrigued me: If Lillie and Tom were involved in an incestuous relationship, their own children could also be each other's cousins. And were there other relations just around the corner, about to make their way to our home? Were we psychologically prepared to host such a family reunion? I kept hearing that refrain in my head, "Please, Lillie, no more kittens."

Lillie neither read my mind nor obeyed my silent appeals: She became pregnant with another litter. I sensed this first because T.J., Perkins, and Miss Tommie formed a protective circle around Lillie at feeding times. Lillie hissed at her children repeatedly when they ate what she considered to be her proprietary food, which amounted to at least twice the amount of her usual helpings. I hoped desperately for a litter consisting of one, an unheard-of statistic, I knew.

The biological clock kept ticking, too, for T.J., Perkins, and Miss Tommie. They were approaching three months old, a safe and appropriate age for spaying and neutering cats. If only this knowledge were so easy to actualize. After caring for them and tending to their needs morning and night, Michael and I were still no closer to taming the three kitties than when we first saw them on that December morning and lent a hand. For Lillie had done what no doubt her own mother had taught her to do: She had taught her kittens to be wary of humans, even those who are seriously intent on helping. All of this meant that we could not pick up the kittens easily, place them inside carriers, and transport them to the veterinarian's office.

The Scoop on...

Trapping Cats—Margarita, Anyone?

The first time is rarely the charm when it comes to trapping an unneutered animal. The old wives' tale about patience being a virtue is highly applicable to this situation. If you are getting ready to trap a cat, you should treat yourself to a glass of fine or better-than-average wine (or the alcoholic beverage of your choice—I like frozen margaritas), grab a terrific book (salacious memoirs rarely disappoint), and sit back in a comfortable armchair. Position yourself by a window or close to a floor-to-ceiling glass door so that you can monitor activity frequently. You could be waiting for hours, possibly for several days. It is as if cats have gone shopping at the local mall and inspected traps before, because when they initially see them—no matter the odd cuts of meat dangling or the tins of smelly tuna tucked inside—they will run faster than jackrabbits. Even short-legged cats can make tracks quickly if they sense that confinement is around the corner. If you fail after several attempts, don't resign yourself to defeat. It is important to remember why you are trapping: The odds have multiplied for your cat to have a longer and healthier life, free of reproductive worries. You might say that the trap is really an unconventionally wrapped gift for your cat.

Best Practices

Dr. O. prepped us on the best practices for trapping feral cats, which is what they were, despite our sustained attempts at domestication. We hatched a plan that required setting three traps, in the front and back of our house and in the driveway, and we attempted to trap the kittens several times, for several weeks. We tried many combinations of food groups to entice them, and nothing worked. Even slices of super-crisp Kentucky Fried Chicken—I'm a Southern girl to the core—were not suitable bait. Michael and I became exasperated and argued about our failed attempts, blaming each other for incompetence. At the office we suppressed emotional outbursts and hid frustrations, but at home we minced no words about our inability to help curtail feline overpopulation.

By contrast, I was becoming expert at cornering delinquent curators about their MIA manuscripts. I warned them of the perils of missed deadlines and the domino effect of their books being no-shows at important exhibition openings attended by top-level donors and influential members of the press. I also had acquired experience as a seasoned counselor, comforting a colleague who, despite her considerable talent, suffered routinely from writer's block. Sadly for her, I knew this impaired state would never be covered under the museum's disability clause.

Feeling blocked or trapped took on a brand-new meaning for me, and my inexperience showed. When I reflect on our trapper days, I wonder how I managed not to buck the experts' recommendations. The requirements for feline trapping are stringent: Deny food overnight or for up to almost two days, as long as the period of deprivation does not lead to a prolonged period of starvation, which might cause injury to the cat's vital organs. A higher power must have been smiling on us in early March because one day we finally caught T.J. and Perkins together in one trap, and we caught Miss Tommie—who in her young life had already begun to do things as she pleased—the following day.

Dr. O. commented on their cuteness, which pleased Michael and me enormously, and for the first time since meeting the kitties, we had to bid them a temporary farewell. Four days later, T.J., Perkins, and Miss Tommie were still recuperating. It turned out that the only way to calm them down, administer their vaccines and rabies shots, and prepare them for spaying/neutering was to put each cat into a pillowcase. This technique would spare them any close encounters of the human kind. Once liberated from the pillowcases, they needed to adjust to the sights of people coming and going in the veterinary clinic.

Back at the ranch, our backyard was empty but for Tom, who took advantage of having the food bowls to himself. Lillie had disappeared in the short time that we had trapped her children, and Michael and I became distressed about her vanishing act. We figured out that she had disappeared to sequester herself underneath our house, where she could have her next litter. We knew this because Lucius kept suspiciously sniffing the floorboards in our living room, and he smelled life underneath the house.

Eight Cats and Counting

Lillie introduced her two male kittens to Michael first. "Diane, you'll never believe this," he exclaimed with pride, as if he himself were the father. Lillie had delivered to us an orange tabby kitten and a brown/black-and-white kitten who was every bit as beautiful as his mother. When I learned of the arrival of another orange tabby, I thought immediately of the name "Leo" and decided that, sight unseen, he would be christened Leo Lucius Lovejoy. Naming him did not mean that I needed to keep him, I assured myself. Michael's description of Leo's brother made me think of the coloring of an acorn. The name Augustus Cornelius, or "Acorn," for short, appealed to me because it was not an old standby, and I was ready to break the mold of using "L" as the first letter of the given names of our cats.

The shuttling between the vet's office, our backyard, and our house proper was exhausting. When we brought T.J., Perkins, and Miss Tommie home, Lillie led the way in teaching her older children to accept her newborns. They all made it look easy, whereas Michael and I were overwhelmed. We needed to integrate the three feline families into our lives, to find a rhythm, to establish some boundaries. What was our ceiling when it came to adopting cats?

We thought we had already reached that number with Lucius, Lydia, Lillie, T.J., Perkins, and Miss Tommie, but we could not help falling in love with Leo and Acorn. With each week, Leo became increasingly rambunctious, merrily chasing his big brother T.J. up and down the driveway. Acorn was already distinguishing himself as an introverted cat who was very attached to Lillie.

At about the six-week mark since their birth, I decided that we couldn't take in more cats permanently. So I created flyers and distributed them at the museum, called cat-loving colleagues, and pleaded with anyone who would listen sympathetically to help us find a good home for Leo and Acorn. My position was that other people could give them a better life than one confined to our backyard.

I could tell that Michael was not pleased when I announced that Laura, a graphic designer at the museum, had offered to adopt Leo and Acorn. She had already told her young daughter about the two kittens and wanted to come to our house to retrieve them. This meant resuming trapping duties immediately, which I dreaded because of the unpredictability. It was hard to forget that my professional career depended on accurate-to-the-letter predictions.

Probably any amateur psychiatrist could have determined whether our inability to trap Leo and Acorn meant our subconscious was sending messages to our pliant minds. The kittens eluded the traps every time we tried, six days straight. Instead of being angry at ourselves, we seemed more accepting of what appeared to be our fate.

Laura was visibly upset when I told her that we could not trap the kittens. "What do you mean you can't? You're the one who knows so much about cats," she stated firmly. I was glad for my untarnished reputation of being knowledgeable about the feline world, but I also felt bad for her. She put me on a guilt trip about how upset her daughter would be. Michael is not a callous person, but I can't say that he was moved by my colleague's story. Wouldn't adopting two more cats complete our lives?

No sooner did we decide to keep Leo and Acorn than I suspected that Lillie was pregnant for a third time. The protective circle of her children that I had observed during Lillie's second pregnancy formed around her again, only now Lillie was encircled by two girls and three boys. This time also was different for another reason. Lillie must have known that she needed to be trapped for her own good. Animals are so smart. Here was a cat who would not let us get too close to her, and then, early one evening, just minutes after he arrived home from work, Michael was able to pick Lillie up for the first time and place her inside a carrier.

We rushed without an appointment to the veterinary clinic, which was beginning to feel like a home away from home, and where sometimes I felt more at ease sparring with the vet techs than I did leading a staff meeting at my own office. Dr. O. acknowledged that Lillie had recently begun another pregnancy. So many cats had come to us at Catland, and we believed they had found their way for a reason. How could we, the head-over-heels cat lovers, sign the paperwork required to terminate a cat's pregnancy? We were advised that Lillie would have given birth to a litter of five kittens, and that we did the right thing, meaning that we had prevented Lillie from being subjected to the unrelenting demands of her reproductive cycles. We couldn't wait to bring Lillie home.

Stormy Weather

What should have been a cause for jubilation about Lillie's future well-being became a conundrum. A dangerous tropical storm was forming nearby in the Gulf of Mexico, and now we, the parents of eight cats, plus the caregivers of a wandering tomcat, were the ones who were trapped. The floodwaters were rising dramatically by the hour around our house, and our driveway became impassable. We called Dr. O. to ask if we could retrieve Lillie the next morning, and we were told to arrive no later than 9:00 a.m. The veterinarian's office had reached its overflow capacity.

No one in Houston saw Tropical Storm Allison coming. My mother called, extremely concerned about whether Michael and I and all of our cats would have time to evacuate. As a native of New Orleans, she knew the drill about escaping on short notice from life-threatening hurricanes.

My mother always bore the responsibility of transporting her children to safety. The television station where my father worked in the French Quarter was only doors away from a luxury hotel, and the station's owner arranged for the families of his employees to take shelter at the Royal Orleans. So my view of hurricanes is admittedly warped. I remember strolling through the hotel's marble-lined lobby while watching the palm trees sway forcefully outside. My mother took my sister and me for dinner in the hotel's famous Rib Room restaurant, where grown-ups ordered steak dinners and martinis served by formally attired waiters. Marcy and I stayed up past our normal bedtimes to watch our father reporting live on TV while the air-conditioner roared comfortably in our make-believe cocoon.

Those days were long gone, and where was my Mommy? I wanted to be a child again, but I could not be mistaken for anyone other than an adult who was terrified of losing everything—Michael and our cats and our house—to a vicious storm.

I was too fidgety to deal with setting traps to secure T.J., Perkins, and Miss Tommie for boarding. Locating and catching Tom also was out of the question. Lucius, a high-strung cat under the sunniest of skies, could not tolerate being boarded, and we knew he would miss Lydia. She was already hiding from the ominous sound of thunder, and I heard her squeal whenever lightning struck close to our house.

Boarding all of the cats was impossible and also did not take into account what I calculated to be Dr. O.'s per diem charges for caring for and feeding eight cats. Evacuating our house, and leaving the cats so that Michael and I could protect ourselves, was unfathomable and would have been unconscionable.

We were an improbable family, destined to ride out the storm together: Michael and I and Lucius and Lydia inside, and all of Lillie's children, and perhaps Tom, too, presumably hiding underneath our old house, tucked in between the nooks and crannies. We were forging a new bond with the cats, one based on our collective survival.

I had plenty of time to think during that harrowing night. Michael was upstairs, channel-surfing for up-to-the-minute weather reports. I sat beside Lucius on the couch in the living room downstairs. Stroking and petting him was a comfort to me, as his preternatural calm soothed my fears of imminent disaster. The brass chandelier and lamp lights kept flickering, though we never lost electrical power. Even with the rain pounding on the leaded-glass

Destiny, Your Name Is Cat

My sister, Marcy, gives me an annual subscription to *Kovels on Antiques and Collectibles*, a monthly newsletter for people who like to collect as well as deal and invest in antiques. One of the articles I liked best is titled "Fated Finds," about the objects that seem to appear out of nowhere but with a specific purpose; they are searching for their new owners. Terry Kovel (a Wellesley woman!) comments specifically on visiting an antiques fair and noticing a silver and citrine brooch by a designer with whom she had worked as a teenage counselor at a summer camp in Maine. Apparently, the brooch had Ms. Kovel in mind, and she obliged by taking her treasured find home to join other pieces in her jewelry collection.

I wasn't officially on the lookout for ten cats to live with Michael and me. So, is it fair to ask what art and antiques collectors and Cat Ladies have in common? There are many similarities that fall into the broad categories of love and obsession and sacrifice. The fundamental differences lie in the calculated moves of an owner to strategically collect and trade objects, compared with the irresistible, often unpredictable ticks of the caregiver's heart to put compassion first, and to watch it triumph. Put another way, while it is customary for collectors to fall in and out of love with the objects they acquire, Cat Ladies do not buy cats in good times and discard them during a credit crunch.

windowpanes, I thought I detected the faint cries of T.J., Perkins, and Miss Tommie. When I put my ear to the floor, I realized that the cats had indeed taken cover below our house. They were standing their ground, staying close to me, in their own way.

Toward the middle of the night, I felt confident that our lives would endure, that I would be able to tell the story of having outlasted this once-in-a-lifetime storm. I could and would continue my journey with the cats.

How was it that I, who labored strictly behind the scenes in my career, and who was considered effective precisely because my editorial intervention was invisible, had become front and center in the eyes of so many felines? There was the menacing eye of the storm hovering above, and then there was I, hunkering down and watching out for the well-being of our cats.

Does the hand that feeds a hungry cat differ significantly from the hand of an editor that assists a hungry author? Hungry can mean famished and starving, or eager and ambitious. In either instance, the hand is extended to help another, and the desire to serve has many unspoken rewards. I was beginning to recognize that my two worlds were not disparate; in fact, they were entwined more than I could have imagined. The key was the connective tissue, making me whole.

Chapter 6

Occupied

Leo

*T*he storm raged on until the early hours of the morning, and I became preoccupied with preserving our cats whose lives were prescribed by the boundaries of the outdoors. Lillie's children had already proved to be troopers, weathering climate changes and withstanding the suffocating humidity for which Houston is unfortunately known. Tropical Storm Allison, however, was more than they had bargained for in their brief existence. As the human leader of the cat pack, I needed to think fast about rescuing these defenseless kitties from nature's fury.

I had earned a reputation as an editor for being resilient, someone who handled manuscript delinquencies and other recurring publishing setbacks without displaying my often deep-seated frustrations. To be resilient meant staying calm, rising above the fracas that often erupted from controversy, and rebounding from roadblocks. I could always gather my thoughts after a dispiriting day at the office and was poised to pounce again by the next workday. I had a cat's killer instinct to emerge a winner after every fight.

Still, I knew that even a little luck could go a long way in overcoming obstacles. And I was one of the lucky ones in life, so it was reasonable to surmise that I could help the cats weather this merciless storm. Fortune had smiled on me consistently with good health, great friends, and an extraordinarily supportive husband and family. Although I had graduated from Wellesley in the late 1970s, I continued to take the college's motto seriously: *Non Ministrari sed Ministrare* ("Not to be ministered unto, but to minister"). I was sufficiently wise in my years to know that I would never win an alumna achievement award for rescuing cats, but I felt fulfilled by my personal cause of ministering to them. The uncertainties of the storm caused me to make an even deeper connection with our feline family. The care and feeding of them also had a silver lining: I was nurturing my soul.

Time was of the essence, and the televised reports continued to be dire: Do not go outside unless to rescue someone. The slick anchormen and affable weathermen were hyped up, and I knew from my father that covering a major storm was a big deal to the on-air personalities, and an automatic ratings bonanza. The talking heads were not into subtleties, and, not that I needed their permission, I thought, "Could 'someone' include a pet"? Michael and I listened to additional reports on the radio, which came through loud and clear: Beware of fire ants and snakes in the swampy water. Michael was not deterred. Despite my desire to help, he insisted that I stay with Lucius and Lydia while he searched for our six cats outside.

Gone Fishin'

Michael pulled on a pair of rarely worn waders and threw on his trusty Barbour jacket, a souvenir from an airport delay in Amsterdam during which he had rewarded his patience with duty-free shopping. He also had grabbed a red-and-white checkered dishtowel, the kind usually draped over the arm of a waiter at a trattoria.

I heard Michael sloshing his way down the driveway toward the street and calling the names of our cats. "Miss Tommie, come out wherever you are. "Perkins, this is Daddy." "T.J., can you hear me?" "Leo and Acorn, do you see me?" "Tom, are you there?" Suddenly I heard a shriek from a cat, a sound so bone-chilling that it could have awakened our neighbors had they not already been upright and transfixed by the televised scenes of people stranded in their cars floating on highways. The cat's outburst was followed by a guttural "damn" from Michael, stumbling through our backyard gate as he tried to hold Leo, who was squirming to escape from the clutches of a human being (the Evil Enemy). Michael had used the dishtowel to wrap Leo in the equivalent of swaddling clothes and was carrying him up the stairs to our garage apartment. When a dripping-wet version of Michael returned to our house, he reported that Leo ran from his grasp to hide in the walk-in closet.

I noticed blood dripping from Michael's left thumb. Apparently, my dearest Leo had bitten my husband. My wifely inclination should have been to look after Michael first and to try and staunch his bleeding. But I was more eager to tend to Leo, sequestered and within range for me to reach out and touch him. The storm prevailed, however, and my turn with Leo would come a day later. Michael opted to nurse his wound by downing a shot of whiskey.

What about Tom and T.J., Perkins and Miss Tommie, and Acorn? Were their fates already determined? Michael thought he saw Acorn hiding inside a tire well of our SUV. Imagining this barely three-month-old kitten clinging to life broke my heart. We had to save him, his siblings, and Tom from drowning.

Hours went by before Tropical Storm Allison finally abated. Houston's drainage system went into high gear as soon as the tide turned, and the waters on our street and in our driveway receded rapidly. When Michael and I felt safe to go outside together, we saw T.J., Perkins, and Miss Tommie walking up the driveway in single file, like ducklings, into our backyard. They looked as if nothing had affected them, and their hardiness amazed me. I could learn from their pliability. With a showman's perfect timing, Tom emerged from underneath our house. He could boast about being the tough guy who had fought the elements and won. And where was our gentle and sweet Acorn?

In the afternoon Acorn arrived unassumingly on the back deck. He looked dazed, rightfully so because he had been left to his own devices for the first time. Acorn began calling pleadingly for Leo, who was still hidden from view in the apartment. I wanted to reunite the two brothers as soon as possible and promised not to let the travails of the storm sever their connection. It was time to resume our sometime occupation as trappers.

Michael had what proved to be an inspired idea, though I was suspicious when I heard about his proposed contraption. He found an old fishing line and hooked a catnip toy onto it. His plan called for suspending the line from the sliding-screen window of the back door and dangling it in front of the trap set squarely in the middle of the deck. Michael bided his time in a folding chair in the mudroom of our house, as if he was going fishing in an imaginary creek that coursed through our backyard and driveway. Assuming that Acorn would eventually bite the bait, then Michael—not known for being an ace fisherman—could entice him to enter the trap. It dawned on me that I had married the mad scientist. Perhaps this was a most fitting union for a madly devoted Cat Lady.

Acorn was so innocent that he had no idea what existed on the other side of the trap. As I watched him approach it without hesitation, I remember thinking, "your life is about to change," and that immensely gratifying thought comes to me every time I rescue a cat. "We got him!" announced Michael triumphantly after only a one-hour fishing trip. Michael and I both carried Acorn (still in the trap) to the apartment to reunite him with Leo. They nestled together and head-bunted with open affection. I was struck again by their bond as littermates.

Relief

The skies remained clear for another twenty-four hours, and the veterinary office reopened to clients lined up to retrieve their pets. We had harbored the romantic notion of a happy reunion with Lillie and were upset to learn that she was despondent and depressed after having been spayed. Once we pulled our car into our driveway, Lillie's radii told her she was home. As soon as we opened the carrier door, Lillie ran around the backyard, initially over the moon and then anxiously searching for Leo and Acorn. I had to guess that, in Lillie's world, it made sense for her to be concerned first for the safety of her newest, and ultimately last, litter.

Lillie walked up and down the deck that she knew so well, pacing back and forth, and a mother's instinct kicked in again. Although she had never observed Michael or me visiting the garage apartment, she sprinted up the stairs and glanced in the windows to see what she could find. If Lillie could talk, I was certain that she would have asked, "Is that where you're keeping my babies?"

I felt guilty for keeping Lillie apart from Leo and Acorn. Was I maybe just a bit—and oddly—jealous of her being their birth mother?

Time seemed to collapse in the days that followed the storm. Michael and I treasured our house even more and were relishing our routines with Lucius and Lydia—from the satisfaction of reading the newspapers on a Sunday morning while sitting by their side, to watching the anticipation on their faces when they heard the familiar sound of a can of cat food opening. We were at their service, and there seemed to be no substitute for the happiness we found with them as well as with our cats who lived outdoors. We would not have traded this unfussy feeling for anything.

We established a new routine with Leo and Acorn. Within an hour after Michael and I returned home from work each day, we checked on them in the apartment. We were thrilled with how easily they had "tamed down," an awkward phrase to an editor's ears but one that meant significant progress to a Cat Lady's way of thinking. I was delighted that Leo and Acorn responded to our touch, both literally and figuratively. Michael and I were contemplating taking a giant leap, moving Leo and Acorn from their temporary apartment into our house permanently. Could these youngsters stand up to Lucius?

The decision to relocate Leo and Acorn was made for us by another disaster. The air-conditioner in the apartment stopped functioning, and I found our two kittens panting from heat exhaustion and gasping for breath. Sophisticated smartphones were rare objects then, and so, instead of texting my state of emergency, I screamed. As I dashed downstairs with Leo, Michael raced up the apartment stairs to gather Acorn into his arms. We were so relieved to rescue them again from harm's way that we forgot to consider a critical factor. The moment of reckoning with Lucius would soon occur.

MySpace, Lucius

I laugh when Lucius saunters into a room. I wonder if, when I'm not looking, he watches DVDs of Westerns and studies cowboys as they size up and stare down their competition. Lucius's reaction to Leo and Acorn was predictable. He smirked and let out a low and polysyllabic hiss. But then he started to growl, which startled me. I had unreasonably hoped that there might be some small space available on Planet Lucius for two adorable and loving kittens to occupy. But territory is territory, and the alpha cat was vocalizing.

Based on the initial botched introduction of Lydia to Lucius, I had already promised myself that, if we ever did this again (famous last words), I would introduce a new cat or cats slowly and properly to the resident cats. I moved

The Scoop on...

Having Happy Holidays with Your Cats

Many of the rules and regulations concerning the safety of cats focus on what we can't give them to play with, especially if they are unsupervised. String and ribbon usually top the precautionary list. So what happens when the holidays arrive every December? Because cats have a precise sense of the change of seasons, they know when you are decorating for and celebrating on special days, whether Christmas, Hanukkah, or Kwanza. Gift wrap and gift boxes fascinate felines, who firmly believe they are the chosen ones who will be receiving your presents. A garland of ribbons is a suitable substitute for a feathered wand, but be sure to watch your cat carefully during the process of entanglement.

Running after your cat running after ribbons can build an appetite—both for you and your cat—and that means it's time for a bountiful reward. When you are preparing your holiday feast, why not coordinate a meal plan for your hungry cats? For example, if your menu includes a traditional turkey, you can't go wrong serving a can of Fancy Feast's turkey giblets to your kitties. If you prefer serving roasted beef tenderloin to the human members of your family, you might try mixing cans of Fancy Feast's chopped grill and tender beef or liver for your feline family. As for setting the perfect holiday table, there is a maker of "kitty china" that offers a unisex serving plate in various colors. Only one word appears, centered in block letters, on the plate: "Spoiled."

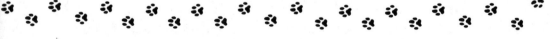

Leo and Acorn into our bedroom, where they would be protected and could acclimate themselves comfortably. Especially after a mentally exhausting day of work at the museum, I looked forward to retreating to our uncluttered bedroom at night—my fortress. But our bedroom began to resemble a showroom for Toys "R" Us. The kittens lacked for nothing, and we could not stop ourselves from indulging them. They played games with each other at all hours, keeping Michael and me awake late at night. Meanwhile, Lucius had graduated to a new level of mind games and wanted to play hardball.

My understanding of "the alpha" is that a cat such as Lucius does not need to show his power because he has it, plain and simple. The alpha cat is respected, though not feared. For Leo and Acorn, Lucius changed up the rules to suit his managerial style. He made sure they knew that he was not going to be fair, or forgiving, and he had never promised that he would be a fun playmate. In our meet-and-greet sessions, Lucius gnawed and chewed and eventually destroyed the kittens' toys. He was not interested in sharing and negotiating. Lucius discerned that Acorn was the meeker of the two kittens, but Lucius was not magnanimous toward Leo, either. Leo did not take no for an answer, putting himself out there as a glad-hander.

I can't believe that we were so cowed by Lucius's conniption fits and contrived reactions that we did not resolve feline tension within the first two weeks of moving Leo and Acorn into our house. Keeping Lucius content was like having another full-time job, and also foremost in our minds was assuring Lydia that, if not the alpha cat, she was at least the second banana.

We were enthralled with the kittens and wanted to give them our undiluted attention. They were growing rapidly, and when we took them to meet Dr. O. and have their routine checkups, she stressed that we needed to have them neutered soonest. Meanwhile, Michael and I were keeping up religiously with our schedule of tending to Lillie, T.J., Perkins, and Miss Tommie outdoors. Tom also was hanging out regularly.

The Art of Caring

How had I arrived at this moment in my life, forming a social network of cats? I had dreamed of becoming a serious art historian and instead had pursued a career that enabled me to edit texts by the leading lights in the galaxy. Was it destiny that each cat had arrived with a distinct purpose, prompting me to enter another realm of art? There is an art to taking care of animals, and the art of sheltering them supplements scientific research. Whereas "warm and fuzzy" and "touchy feely" are terms used sparingly in art books, the art of caring for animals absolutely depends on going with your gut, doing what you know to be best for your pet. Touching, feeling, and offering your heart are natural impulses. With the adoption of each cat, I was learning that the art of feline living was an intuitive genre unto itself.

On the morning of the day that became known as 9/11, I turned on the TV in our bedroom at the exact moment when the second jetliner hit the twin tower of the World Trade Center. Michael had already left for work, and I called him at his office to ask if he was aware of the horrific breaking news. Michael's assistant had just received a phone call and had turned on the portable TV in their office, so Michael knew. His voice was shaky, and Leo and Acorn must have sensed the fear in my own voice because they hopped on the bed, close to where I was sitting. Michael recommended that I go to work, to act as if life was normal despite chaos, because—according to the televised reports—that was the advice of the moment. Perhaps the museum's security staff had received top-level information with which to debrief employees. I also was very concerned about the well-being of my staff.

As soon as I reached the office, I learned that there was no reassuring information to be shared. I remember staring blankly at the paperwork stacked neatly on my desk, the manuscripts prioritized by time-sensitive urgency. I prided myself on maintaining a tidy workspace, but this feeling seemed even more trivial in the face of terrorism. Houston, the energy capital of the world, was an easy target. If Americans were being blown up, and Michael's and my turn had come, then the only scenario I could accept was for us to be taken out at once as a family, with all of our cats. I recommended that everyone on my staff go home: Work could wait.

I left my office quickly, eager to meet Michael at home and to hibernate. We clung to our safety, especially in the days and weeks immediately following 9/11. Early in December, we finally liberated Leo and Acorn from their forced isolation. We would face the new world, whatever its constitution, together, not in seclusion.

There wasn't exactly mayhem in our household, but Lucius and Lydia were far from pleased with having new family members. Our festive seasonal decor provided a modest diversion from the tragedy of 9/11. In our small corner of the world at Catland, the holidays, especially in 2001, needed to be even more about caring and giving. This was not the gospel according to Lucius. But Leo became our cat who loved Christmas, and I took such pleasure in watching him get into the holiday spirit as Michael and I pulled out the boxes of vintage ornaments (another collecting fetish of mine). We needed Leo to believe in miracles that year. We didn't see much of Acorn after we released him from captivity in our bedroom. Acorn spent most of his days dodging Lucius—a sensible strategy that Michael and I completely understood.

Move-ins

The additional expenses that typically arrive with the holidays caused me to think that Michael and I could use some extra income. In the wake of 9/11, preserving the lives of our cats was paramount, and it could be helpful to offset the mounting costs of caring for so many four-legged friends. I was a reality TV series waiting to happen—"Cat Lady Plus Eight, and a Wandering Tom"— and I imagined camera crews following me as our kids ate us out of the house. Animal Planet, here we come!

I overheard Beth, a young female colleague in my office, talking about wanting to rent a garage apartment in the vicinity of the museum. Ours was unoccupied, which meant instant income. Although Michael didn't mind cats peering at us through the glass doors, he resisted the idea of leasing because he was still clinging to some vague notion of privacy. But I already accepted that when you're joined at the hip with cats, "linked in" with them, privacy no longer enters into the equation. So I got my way with Michael.

Having a human tenant meant still more responsibilities. There were tedious IRS forms for rental income to prepare in time for tax returns, and I made frequent calls to electricians to re-lube the air-conditioning condenser that we had been assured was repaired after Leo's and Acorn's near death. Keeping Beth happy and the apartment occupied translated into a supplemental monthly income of $350, and that satisfied my lust for money.

I also noticed that Leo had a thing for blondes. Every weekday morning, as Beth bound down the stairs to head for work, Leo ran to the glass doors and shamelessly flirted with her, whereas Lillie, Tom, T.J., Perkins, and Miss Tommie rebuffed Beth's advances. Whenever they saw Beth, they acted like obstinate feral cats, rushing from the comfort of their heating pads—which, I have on the highest authority, most feral cats do not have—and hiding.

As a compulsive list-maker, I always keep tally of my New Year's resolutions so that I can document my personal and professional goals. The beginning of 2002 was particularly reflective because of the aftereffects of 9/11. What did I want to be in life? What did I aim to accomplish to make a difference and an impact? I was a career woman and a wife, and I was also knee-deep in being Cat Lady, who was proving to be a career woman in her own right. I needed to gather my wits while tending to the move-ins and everything else that revolved around me.

With one hand I was feeding two cats and with the other hand grooming another two; I was changing four litter boxes and sprinkling catnip on carpets along the way; I was restocking the outdoor feeding stations for five cats and setting their heating pads on the high-comfort level. And then there was my day job, at which my boss kept upping the ante as the museum intensified its publishing program, per the trustees' unanimous investment in the written word.

In the back of my mind, I heard the voice of reason: This Is It. If I saw another stray cat in the backyard, I would have to turn a blind eye. The irony was not lost on me. I worked in a profession that required having a trained eye. Could I really pretend not to see? When I described the incremental challenges of home life to my colleagues at work, I found myself—who had once sworn on *The Chicago Manual of Style* to honor and obey the English language—abusing it. I was taking liberties, joking that Michael and I had reached what Heather, a fellow editor and friend, had cleverly termed our maximum feline "catpacity." She remarked that I was an editor who "pursued 'litter-ary' endeavors with a special touch." I appreciated her humor, especially during this mournful period of American life, and cat jokes were an innocent form of escape. Many officemates teased me about my cat family, while some simply shrugged their shoulders. Many more would chime in unison: Downsize. But I could never lighten my presumed load. No one had forced me to fall in love with felines.

Unexpected Heartbreak

It was easy to adore Leo and Acorn. They were kind cats whose only sign of possible ferocity was evidenced in their strapping size, especially those supersized paws that sprung into action whenever I tossed toys onto our bed. By the spring of 2002, Leo had coerced his way into Lucius's life, and Lucius had begrudgingly accepted him. Acorn was integrating himself in his usual, non-confrontational manner. One day I noticed that he seemed unnaturally still. I teased him, "come here, Mr. Acorn," as I liked to call him. When he walked toward me, his body seemed to be suspended in motion. Over the next few days Acorn did not have much of an appetite, and the fur he had shed from his winter coat was desiccated. Leo groomed him often, as if to reassure him, "Whatever is wrong, I'll make it okay."

I had scheduled a lunch with Karen, a close friend and colleague who also loves cats. She had recently lost her oldest cat to chronic renal failure, and when I told her about my worries for Acorn, she suggested that he was probably too young to be inflicted with a life-threatening illness. I left the lunch feeling relieved but also cognizant of one of Michael's favorite phrases, "Beware of the pit god." I wasn't about to get too full of myself with false optimism, and then be knocked down. We had survived our baptism-by-fire initiation into the feline world, and we were still in the early stages of life with our cats. I had to believe that we would be spared heartbreak. I reminded myself that Acorn had passed all of his first veterinary tests without any cause for alarm.

I continued to monitor Acorn rather obsessively. Scrutinizing him was different from the way I study the personalities of the museum's curators. To perform editorial surgery on a manuscript requires understanding an author's needs and objectives and tolerance level for accepting suggestions. Although a book can be a definitive source of wisdom and a key to unraveling mysteries, I could not bear to consult a textbook about feline illness. I feared confronting the truth about Acorn's condition. I also could not cling to hope that his apparent illness would resolve itself. Though Acorn, like most cats, was adept at hiding discomfort, I sensed his pain and brought him to Dr. O.'s attention on a rush basis. The moment I handed Acorn to the veterinary technician, I had a bad feeling. She tagged his carrier with the code "ADR." "What's that?" I asked. "Ain't doin' right," she replied. In better times, I would have playfully scolded the vet tech for her poor grammar, but I kept my mouth shut and accepted her frank response.

I didn't wait long to receive Acorn's official diagnosis. The veterinary office called on the same day that I left Acorn for observation. One of Dr. O.'s veterinary colleagues said that, if Michael and I chose to research Acorn's condition, we might want to do so with stiff drinks in hand. Acorn was diagnosed with a fatal viral disease named feline infectious peritonitis (FIP). The rate of occurrence is about one in five thousand for a household with one or two cats. Michael and I could try to make Acorn more comfortable in the days ahead, as there would not be weeks or months by which we could measure our remaining time with him.

I tried to be brave at the office on that unbearable day. No one ever had seen me cry at work, despite the low points that blipped on my professional horizon from time to time. I headed to my car and phoned Michael. By the time he answered the call, I was sobbing. I conveyed everything I knew about the cruel, uncommon disease afflicting Acorn, and I concluded our conversation with the stark fact that there were no favorable odds.

We were able to sustain Acorn for fourteen days. I made a consistent effort to put on my game face at the office, and I was especially concerned that Dr. Marzio might see me in a vulnerable state. He and I had once conducted business over lunch, instead of over his conference table, and midway through the meeting he asked why I had pursued editing. I probably replied in an unemotional tone to appear businesslike, whereas I should have felt free to describe why it matters that experts have a forum for publishing their findings and opinions on art. In my annual reviews, Dr. Marzio had evaluated me as being unflappable and always engaged in the subject matter assigned. What if I started crying about Acorn in the middle of a meeting with the museum's director? There goes my credibility.

Because of Acorn's situation, I lacked the desire and could not summon the energy to participate in any stimulating discussion, especially about art. After 9/11, I wrote several general-purpose texts, circulated to the museum's membership, in which I described the restorative and healing power of art. Ironically, I no longer believed my own words. Everything clicked when all of the cats were healthy. I had never considered an alternative scenario. I had to reserve my emotional strength for Acorn.

He was losing weight precipitously and could not eat much. We bottle-fed him with a vitamin-rich formula given to a kitten, and we brought him to Dr. O.'s office for subcutaneous fluids. Michael and I dreaded these trips, as we didn't know if we would return home with or without Acorn. He could barely jump onto a chair or our bed. We were advised to sequester him, even though the disease was not contagious to humans or to our other cats.

I moved into our guest bedroom so that I could sleep next to Acorn at night. Although he was declining rapidly, I refused to think of him as sickly. But Leo and Lucius and Lydia smelled sickness, and they knew that something was out of whack. Lydia's survivor instinct kicked in and she parked herself outside the bedroom, hissing at the weak victim who must have known that Lydia was lurking. Lucius was equally cruel, though silently. He had no interest in checking on Acorn. That left our soulful Leo, whom I could hear meowing periodically during the night.

Sometimes, in the middle of the night, I heard Acorn nibble on a few pieces of dry food and then groom himself. One night, there was only stillness. I looked at the end of the bed, where Acorn slept faithfully at my feet, and I felt his tiny body. He could not have weighed more than five pounds, and his abdomen was heaving up and down. I stayed awake the rest of the night to watch for a more intense sign of life.

Michael and I had avoided talking about Acorn's inevitable death. Michael felt strongly that Acorn should have the right to die in our home, the only one that he had known. I disagreed and argued that Acorn should be allowed to die with his beauty and his dignity intact, which would require euthanizing him. Allowing him to suffer would constitute gross negligence on our part. We both understood that the FIP disease would cause him to suffocate to death.

On May 1, 2002, I made the most agonizing decision of all. When I awakened that morning, I realized that I had not heard Acorn eating or grooming himself the night before. I looked frantically for Acorn, who was hiding in a corner of the bedroom. I brought him some food, which he refused. When I tried to pick him up, his body went completely limp.

I called Dr. O. as soon as the veterinary office opened and inquired about euthanizing Acorn. Michael and I placed him in a carrier and walked slowly through the house, talking softly to Acorn and pausing at certain places where he always liked to sit and observe the life of the street—children riding bikes, teenagers Rollerblading, and couples walking dogs. As the three of us proceeded to my car, Michael stopped for a few moments in our backyard, pointing to the spot where we first laid eyes on Acorn.

Cat Magnet

On the rare occasion that I travel far from Catland, I discover that cats know where to find me. This discovery does not require my possessing the research skills of an intrepid curatorial assistant. When I visited the home of Mary, my Wellesley roommate, in Minneapolis, it was impossible to get a good first-night's sleep. That's because Jason, her supposedly unfriendly bruiser of a grey tabby cat, crept into the guest bedroom where I was staying. Put bluntly: Jason wanted to sleep with me on our first date. The room was festooned with pretty pink decorations fit for a fairy-tale princess and decked out with a four-poster canopied bed. Midway through the night, I heard the door creak open as Jason waddled his way into the bedroom. He crash-landed on top of the canopy before descending on to the mattress, clumsily positioning his body close to mine.

The next morning, when Mary asked if I had slept comfortably, I suggested she rephrase the question. "Do you mean did Jason and I enjoy our special evening together?" I was not surprised to learn that Jason had never snuggled next to Mary's other houseguests before, regardless of their college affiliation. Later that day, Jason came back for more. He communicated, by repeatedly rubbing up against my legs, "You're a cat magnet."

Our final drive with Acorn to Dr. O.'s office was utterly quiet. I was driving the equivalent of a funeral hearse, a situation I could have avoided, but I couldn't bear to watch Acorn draw his last breath at our house. Michael and I were given some private moments with Acorn in the examination room before we knocked on the door and signaled that the time had come for Dr. O. to enter. We kissed and stroked Acorn's head and thanked him for gracing our lives for thirteen months. We told him he had put up a very courageous fight. We lacked the courage to watch him die.

As soon as Michael and I returned home, I called my office and said that I could not come to work. I didn't offer any excuse except that I had decided on the spur of the moment to take a personal day. Michael also stayed home and tried not to think about what, he said, "I had made him do to Acorn." My rational self told me that Acorn was untreatable, that our euthanizing him was the most humane means of liberating him from further suffering. My emotional self struggled with thinking that perhaps Michael was right, that we, the couple who could not have enough cats, had elected to kill one of our own.

I wasn't eager to clean up Acorn's belongings in the days that followed his death, yet I returned often to the guest bedroom—temporarily his room—to touch his blankets and toys, wanting to smell his lingering scent. For sanitary reasons, I needed to remove the contents of his litter box and to sterilize the room as soon as possible.

Leaving a Void

People say that there is no greater grief for a parent than that of losing a child. Even though I have never given birth, I understand this visceral feeling of grief because of having lost Acorn. Not a day goes by that I do not think of this precious cat who lived on earth for far too brief of a spell. We keep Acorn's ashes in a handsome antique leather box that is tucked inside the top drawer of Michael's dresser. I believe in a heaven above, and I hope that Acorn is resting peacefully.

Some people also say that the void of losing a loved one cannot be filled. Prior to Acorn's passing, I could count on one hand the number of my family members and friends who had died. When I thought about death, which was not often—especially when I was young—I thought about it in abstract terms. I had studied many paintings of people who were on the cusp of dying, and, like most people, I gravitated toward artists' depictions that were serene and ennobling rather than bloody and gruesome. Acorn's death forced me to recognize that I had been sheltered for too long from confronting the reality of mortality.

I didn't suffer from any physical ailments after Acorn's death, the way I did after Aunt Susan was killed in a car accident and my legs cramped so severely that I couldn't sleep at night for nearly a year. The pain from losing Acorn was almost as acute, though this time centered in my head. I wasn't interested in attending pet-grief support sessions to talk openly about mourning Acorn's death. I renewed my unspoken vow to respect the sanctity of our cats' lives, knowing firsthand that there were no guarantees for longevity.

I also learned from Acorn's death that no matter the tensions at the office, I would never deal with life-or-death issues there. I needed to get a firmer grip on taking the slings and arrows of publishing misfortune in my stride. Like a stray cat, I had become accustomed to late-night hours of roaming and hunting, and my reward was manuscript bits and pieces. Now I ignored the original stringent due dates I had dictated and was willing to assemble the texts without the clock ticking. Editing began to seem easier; my recommendations to the curators came to mind quickly. I was loosening up, becoming more tolerant of colleagues' quirks and foibles, just as I was accepting my own. Naturally, I couldn't announce myself to the world as Cat Lady the moment I emerged from my mother's womb, so it wasn't fair for me to expect every curator to be a born writer.

One of the most intellectual writers at the museum commented that she admired my ability to keep the multiple book projects on track despite the "conflicting personality issues," as she termed them. This curator has one of the best eyes in the business, and she observed that I seemed less conflicted with myself. She followed up with a note, "You have an analytical mind working with a kind heart." A love token such as this one from a curator to an editor would have been nearly unthinkable in my pre-Cat Lady days.

I had what can best be described as an "aha!" moment, though without the fanfare that accompanied this kind of revelation on Oprah's TV shows. I was relating better to people because of my ability to relate to cats. Being a dedicated Cat Lady was enabling me to thrive as a more considerate editor. Conversely, being a detail-obsessed editor was helping me to flourish as an attentive Cat Lady. I took another vow, which was to thank my lucky stars for being surrounded by rich personalities of the human and the feline persuasion.

Shortly after Acorn's death, I began editing a multiauthored book on Latin American avant-garde art in which I kept encountering a phrase that was in vogue with the cognoscenti: "the void of plenitude." I queried each of the authors, not about varying the phrase to avoid repetition but about explaining the meaning of these seemingly contradictory words. Before too long, I came to my own conclusion.

The void in my life, left by the premature departure of Acorn, could be filled with a plenitude of cats. We did not need to look far and wide for more cats. Lillie and Tom, T.J., Perkins, and Miss Tommie were living together in close proximity in our backyard. We could undoubtedly extend their life spans by moving them indoors. If I could find potential in broken antiquated pots, then surely I could tap the potential of these living creatures.

I wouldn't need to save money to send my "kiddy-cats" to college. They were street smart, literally, possessing an innate intelligence. I knew I could learn more than a thing or two from them. It was easy to sense their magic, which was not alchemic or cosmic, or the kind of voodoo magic that permeates the streets of New Orleans. This was old-fashioned magic, the kind that inspires unequivocal love.

Filling the Void

Fast-forward to December 1, 2002, when I, Landlord, formally notified Beth, Tenant, that Michael and I were increasing her rent. There was no other choice for us to manage the fluctuating costs of fuel and Freon to keep the apartment habitable. She declined to renew at the higher fixed monthly rate, and despite my previous desire to hoard extra cash, I didn't force the issue. Had I wanted to evict Beth because of a new twist in the plot I was hatching to fill the void?

I would toss caution to the wind, reverse course, and spend the extra rental income we had earned to provide for Lillie and Co. How irrational was that? I bet the museum's comptroller would wag her finger at me, eventually smiling after I explained my personal theory of accountability: The principles of accounting do not matter to Cat Lady. Michael and I would "lease" the apartment to Lillie, T.J., Perkins, and Miss Tommie for free. If we could ever catch Tom and have him neutered, there would be a party of five.

I could not wait to tell Michael that it was his turn to get his way, that he would never see another human being live in the apartment again. Yet I could proudly re-hang the shingle on the apartment's front door: Occupied!

Chapter 7

Linus

Enticed

"Occupied" and "spoiled" were two of the top words that recurred in my lexicon as Cat Lady, and joining them was "meow." No other word came close to packing such a wallop, given that only two syllables—*me* and *ow*—conveyed so much. Although I resist snippets and frown on awkward contractions as an editor, I endorse meow for its meaningful brevity. I love listening to the different intonations of our cats' meows as they open their tiny mouths to make their voices heard.

A substantial portion of my professional work depends on making voices heard, be they the artist's voice published in documents and manifestos and treatises, or the curatorial voice that resonates in keenly detailed analyses and evocative descriptions of works of art. A discovery of an artist's voice that surfaces in a once-lost manuscript is a euphoric moment that often sets the art world on fire. A fresh voice in the literary world is equally prized. From living in Texas, I am partial to the sounds of both the lilting drawl and the charming twang (and Michael's yee haws!). The numerous feline voices I hear at home would not make headlines, nor could they be categorized by region or defined by accent. Yet the lives of our cats depend completely on communication, and on my understanding the cats' wishes and demands. ·

Because Lucius, Lydia, Lillie, Leo, T.J., Perkins, Miss Tommie, and Tom each issued a distinctive meow, it was easy for me, one morning, in January 2003, to discern that I was listening to another meow—an unknown voice—coming from a cat who was extremely determined to be heard. This was not a strong or bellowing voice; instead, the voice was pleading. What was I hearing? "Hello?" "Will you feed me?" "Can I come live with you?" I knew the definitive answer before even putting a face to a voice and giving a name to the face. The answer was all of the above.

Psychic Powers

I had dreamed of the undersized orange tabby kitten at our back door. The night before I first saw the stray kitty whom I would name Linus Thomas Lovejoy, I had fallen asleep frustrated after a long day at the office of dealing with some of the museum's fiercest egos. In my dream, Michael and I had a heated argument about our feline family. Just like couples debating the pros and cons of having another child, I had put my foot down with Michael, insisting that we could no longer take in lost or stray cats arriving in our backyard. In my dream, I told him, "You talk a good game, but I'm not stupid. If you see a little orange kitten, you'll cave." I casually forgot to inform him that I would be right there beside him, in real time.

Was I becoming Psychic Cat Lady? I couldn't believe that I was seeing my dream fulfilled. How much should I charge for my consultations with fellow cat lovers, and would I specialize in palm or Tarot card readings? But before establishing this new practice, I opened the door to the backyard inconspicuously and tiptoed onto the deck. First I had to alert Michael, to whom I called out in my most urgent-sounding voice: "There is an orange kitten in our backyard, and I dreamed about one last night."

Once I moved past the state of astonishment over my newfound psychic powers, I focused on the embodiment of my dream. As orange cats go, Lucius is considered handsome and Leo a beauty, but this orange kitten did not have a pretty or even a good-looking face and fit more into the category of an ugly duckling. I could see easily that the kitten was a male, and I guessed he was probably nearing four months old. He had green eyes, and both his face and body were horribly thin. He had Fu Manchu–style whiskers, and the patches of white underneath his chin, combined with his orange fur, called to mind the coloring of a Creamsicle, my favorite childhood treat.

The kitten's legs were very short, and the length of my index finger matched the length of one of his legs. His paws were enormous, just like Lillie's and her children's, and especially relative to his small size. The orange kitten had rough and calloused paws, and his medium-length fur was flea-bitten. When I tried to reach out and pet the kitty newcomer, he scampered as fast as he could through our backyard and into an alleyway behind our house.

The last thing that Michael and I needed was another cat. We were not looking to replace Acorn, who was irreplaceable in our minds. We also had devised our strategy for trapping Lillie, T.J., Perkins, and Miss Tommie, and we could not entertain any other feline distraction. The task at hand required military precision: 1–2–3–4, and then we would have achieved moving the "outside, downstairs" cats to their "inside, upstairs" existence. But we also had not built impenetrable fortresses around our hearts.

We kept hearing the meows of Linus, who, just like his namesake from the *Peanuts* cartoon, needed a security blanket to protect him. We watched Linus approach our back door early in the morning, trying to get to the food bowls and chow down before Lillie and her daughters arrived to chase him away. They wanted to have fun, at his expense, and I couldn't blame them for zealously guarding their food source. T.J. was non-confrontational toward Linus, and when Tom showed up, he surprised us by not being threatened by Linus, either.

This routine ensued for a few weeks, and one morning after Linus jumped our backyard fence, he proceeded to our neighbor's backyard instead of to the alleyway. The young couple next door had just welcomed a baby boy to their family, and they had bribed their two-year-old son to behave by giving him a playground-worthy jungle gym. The child in Linus must have recognized that this fanciful and colorful structure could provide a perfect hiding spot from neighborhood bullies—Lillie's girls.

Linus continued to come and go each day in January, inching closer to Michael and me when we restocked the food bowls. I started to cave, in keeping with my dream. It was chilly outside then—at least for Houston's mild winters—and I worried that a kitten as tiny as Linus would feel the cold penetrating his thin bones.

How could Linus feel comfortable sleeping outside at night? Did he perhaps tuck himself inside the base of a tree trunk? Did he discover a yard down the street from our house, where he could curl up in a stack of leaves to stay warm? Did he play possum underneath our or someone else's house, or underneath a car?

Linus started brushing up against my legs in the morning hours. He never lowered the decibel level of his meows, and he added physical contact to the mix. The closer I got to him, the more I realized that he was developing the cabbage-shaped head of a tomcat, and that he looked very much like an orange version of Tom. Could Linus be another one of Tom's progeny?

I put this hypothetical to Michael, who was having marvelous fun reminding me that I had sworn off cats in my recent dream. He, too, had become fascinated by watching Linus, and if silence is golden, then Michael could swear on that oath. They were communicating telepathically, and I would not have put it past Michael to convey to Linus, "Keep working on her, she's Cat Lady."

The Parent Trap

Our work was still cut out for us with Operation Trap and Move. I knew we had made the right decision to relocate Lillie and her children to the vacant (or, as Michael gloated, unoccupied-by-a-human) garage apartment, even though the decision was, you might say, an unorthodox one. But there was no going back on the path of commitment to our cats, no room for reneging, even if all roads kept leading to a lifestyle that looked conventional wisdom in the eye and said, "Thanks, but no thanks." When some of my colleagues at the museum described how hard it was for them to find a rental property that allows pets, I did not say a word. What might they think about my mental competence if I revealed that I was relinquishing our rental-worthy apartment to four cats? In my new role as a benevolent landlord, I would allow our pets to have an apartment for themselves. In lieu of a security deposit, I would deposit them— as it were—in the security of their own home.

I had cleaned the five-hundred-square-foot apartment thoroughly in preparation for the cats' arrival, and when Lillie fell into the trap, Michael and I made tracks. As I opened the door to welcome our first tenant, I was struck by the gleaming white walls and windowsills, and the freshly scrubbed white tile floors. The sand-colored Berber carpet in the living room and the bedroom was free of dust bunnies, and the all-white bathroom—a pair of vanities, a toilet, and a shower/tub stall—was immaculate. This setup was a far cry from White Cube, the white, two-tier gallery in London that is famous for presenting challenging, often shocking exhibitions of contemporary art. But I was still proud of this white cube of an apartment and of achieving a new state of housekeeping nirvana. Despite maintaining a neatnik's desk at work, I was not known for being Martha Stewart at home. I never had sufficient time on the weekends—or so I told myself—to devote to major cleaning that would pass the white-glove test. But for Lillie and her ward, I demanded nothing short of perfection.

Lillie was curious, more so than scared, when we released her from the trap, and she seemed pleased with the creature comforts readily available to her. She walked around the apartment as if she was mentally verifying her list of must-haves. Cat trees and scratching posts, check! Bowls for food and water, check! Toys, check! Night-lights, check! I furnished the apartment with a contemporary oak kitchen table and a set of four Windsor-style chairs from Pottery Barn. The cats' bedroom consisted of a card table and a futon mattress, on which I arranged several color-coordinated fleece blankets and decorative felt pillows from Ikea. I programmed the radio to play continuous classical music. The central heat was functioning well, and, thanks to the new airtight insulation in the apartment, the place felt comfortable. Lillie had to know she had it good. In fact, Lillie was living in better style, surrounded by more square footage, than I had when I moved into my first studio as a single woman trying to establish myself in New York City.

Next in line for relocation was T.J. He, too, was a remarkably easy touch, and we reunited him with Lillie only a day after she had set her four paws on carpet and tile for the first time. When we brought T.J. inside the apartment, he walked about with assurance, as if he had orchestrated the move himself. Lillie head-bunted and groomed him, and when I called out, "What do you say, T.J.?" I think he responded, "Works for me." From observing T.J. and interacting with him outdoors, I had come to the conclusion that he was a simple-minded cat. This innocence worked to his advantage in the relocation. What might have been a radical upheaval for one cat was just another day in the life of easygoing T.J.

Two down, two to go with Operation Trap and Move, and leave it to Perkins and Miss Tommie to challenge me and my husband, the self-titled kitty commandos. Michael wanted to reactivate the "gone fishin'" mechanism he had designed to

The Scoop on...

Scoping Cat Decor

There is a saying that you don't have to spend a lot to have good taste. You also don't need to have good taste to spend a lot. When it comes to decorating a home for cats, there truly is no accounting for personal taste, anyway. So go for it, and a good place to begin your shopping spree is at resale stores.

These stores, along with thrift shops and dollar emporiums, are a gold mine for vintage wares, retro trinkets, and just plain "junque" related to our favorite pet. When I was foraging for items for our cats' garage apartment, I was initially overwhelmed by the volume of gently distressed and previously used merchandise for sale. I almost felt as if the damaged goods were commentary on the plight of abandoned pets. But the more cups and saucers and candleholders and lamp stands that I saw, the more I realized that my love of cats is shared by millions. Collecting cat memorabilia is a way of declaring your pride in the species. And when your feline census has reached its limit, whatever that number may be, don't despair. Your universe of cats can continue to expand, thanks to the humorous, playful, and often unabashedly tacky objects that are classified as cat decor. Curators won't come near this stuff, and don't even think of mentioning the subject with any degree of seriousness to an art book publisher.

trap Acorn, whereas I suspected that Perkins was too smart to walk unwittingly into such a ludicrous trap. Miss Tommie, still the smallest cat of Lillie's first litter, hid under our house for the majority of each day. I was concerned that even the pungent smell of fresh tuna or salmon would not lure her from her semi-subterranean existence, enticing her to enter the trap at free will.

I requested days off from work to try to catch the ever-elusive Perkins and Miss Tommie. Although Dr. Marzio was not the kind of boss who micromanaged and breathed down the necks of his employees, I still needed to comply with the official requests from the human resources department to complete absentee forms. "Personal business" sounded faintly mysterious; I flattered myself thinking that Dr. Marzio wondered what his mild-mannered editor was doing in her spare time. "Trapping cats" sounded too bizarre, so I cheated and wrote "doctor appointment" each time to support my requests. And Dr. Marzio signed off perfunctorily, never crossing the line to ask whether I was consulting a dentist or a shrink, and never guessing that my primary-care provider was a veterinarian.

Michael set up the traps early in the morning, and I sat by the back door for hours, trying to be patient. But I was fuming. I had to earn a living, and these two cats were playing mind games with us—not quite on Lucius's manipulative level, but close. Perkins and Miss Tommie approached the trap, circled and inspected it carefully, put their noses inside to smell the fish, and then turned away haughtily. Perkins once looked at me as if to say, "Duh, I've been spayed already." Although I didn't want to deprive Perkins and Miss Tommie of sustenance for too long, I felt desperate when it appeared that we would never trap them and move them indoors.

Michael agreed to join me for a day off at home, on the last day of February, and Perkins must have guessed that it was time for closure. Enough of experimenting with food—Michael rigged the trap with catnip. That sleight of hand was all we needed. But when the trap door snapped shut, Perkins freaked out. She was hissing and writhing inside the trap, and I was afraid that Michael would drop it en route to the apartment because of her gesticulations and gyrations. Once set free inside the apartment, Perkins became so flustered that she began to pant heavily. I had never seen a cat hyperventilating before, and luckily my instincts kicked in. I sat on the cool tile floor in the kitchen, and miraculously Perkins followed suit—chilling, physically and figuratively.

The next few days were touch–and–go with Perkins. She wanted out. I couldn't abandon our plan to domesticate her, her siblings, and Lillie. Surely Perkins would come around to accepting the predictability of her new life, one that lacked in excitement but offered full-time stability and an outpouring of love in exchange.

Perkins acclimated during the month of March. Perhaps she was resigned to her fate, or perhaps, because she was smart, she had figured out this new deal. Miss Tommie was the lone holdout. I couldn't withhold her food for more than two days, to essentially threaten her—enter the trap or else, Miss Tommie. We tried trapping her three times a week, leaving our weekends to gear up for the next week of attempts. With each effort, Miss Tommie walked away, head held high and defiantly. Michael and I thought we would be forced to keep her outside, where she might even befriend Linus. She would also have her father, Tom, for occasional company. Then, unexpectedly one evening, the god of winter weather returned to smile on Michael and me.

Oh, What a Night

March is one of the most glorious months of the year in Houston. Azaleas of blazing pink and fuchsia intensity are in full bloom, the temperature is mild, the humidity is low, and the pollen count is manageable. A freakish cold spell hit the city, and on March 29—I remember the date well—I noticed that Miss Tommie was trying to stay warm outside on the doormat. Could this be our golden opportunity? She had been separated from her mother and siblings for nearly three months, and she needed a real home, not one that amounted to living underneath our house. We could do better for her. But if we opened the back door and brought out the trap, in broad view under the intense glare of the flood lights, she would run for cover. I didn't allow myself to dream another dream of a kitty rescue, and so I went upstairs to watch TV.

About an hour later I heard a groaning noise, and the voice in need could belong only to that of a cat. I ran downstairs to find that Michael had closed the sliding door between our kitchen and the mudroom. I whispered through the door, "What is going on?" He replied calmly, "I've got Miss Tommie."

I opened the door narrowly and crawled into the mudroom. There she was, crouching on a wool throw rug, hugging her body tightly for warmth and presumably to allay her fears. But how could we move her from point A in our house to point B in her new house, and in the cold darkness of the night? Miss Tommie needed to chill. What was it about cats that brought out antiquated slang in me? I couldn't get away with using slang in editorial work, but "chill" was the correct word of the hour.

I'm not convinced that Miss Tommie was ready for the move. She was trapped between two doors, one behind her—a means of egress to her previously liberated life—and one several feet away, closer to where I was kneeling on the floor. Thank heaven that no one from the museum saw me in this abject state. I had always joked that I would never get down on my hands and knees to solicit an overdue manuscript.

Miss Tommie did not take pity on me doing my best to behave like a four-legged creature, to be a copycat. I felt incredible relief when I coaxed her into the tried-and-true carrier that had transported T.J. to the apartment. Yet Michael and I were slightly jittery on our feet, unsure of the reunion that was about to occur.

Bookworm

It had not crossed my mind that Miss Tommie's mother and her two siblings would reject her. When we released Miss Tommie from the carrier, she ran to hide behind a bookshelf, which I had stocked with publications by some of my favorite literary lions: short stories by William Faulkner and John Updike, plays by Tennessee Williams, poems by Wallace Stevens, mysteries by Raymond Chandler, and novels by Barbara Pym. Maybe Miss Tommie, just like me, was seeking refuge in the comfort of books.

For several days and nights, Miss Tommie rotated her hiding place in the apartment. I had not filed the books methodically on the bookshelf like a librarian—there was no rhyme or reason to the stacking—but it was interesting to note that Miss Tommie made the literary rounds, from the highest shelf to the lowest one. There had always been a certain strict quality to her appearance, and I could imagine Miss Tommie wearing bifocals, poring over books late at night. Books were her safety net, and the random display of the tightly packed books prevented the other cats from approaching Miss Tommie wherever she hid on or behind a particular shelf. Because she had lived outdoors longer than the other members of her family, she smelled different from them and had developed a tougher street ethic that alienated Lillie, T.J., and Perkins, despite their blood relation. I think Miss Tommie had told herself that she could live independently and would be fine surviving without her family. But the door to the apartment remained locked, preventing escape.

Time always proves to be the great healer. Although the first few weeks of Miss Tommie's reunion with her family were not filled with bliss, the four cats began to adjust and to stake their claims in the apartment. I wondered if I opened the door—the door to their freedom—would they all run out at once? I hated to think of them as kidnap victims or shut-ins. One or two might stay behind, appreciative of their indoor-only environment.

I also never considered Lillie and her family to be second-class citizens, not quite good enough to live with Michael and me. My decision to move them into the garage apartment was influenced by the number of cats we already had living inside the house with us, and knowing that commingling the two families might be more than we could handle without quitting our professional jobs and becoming full-time cat-family referees.

Just as Lillie, T.J., Perkins, and Miss Tommie had realigned their lives successfully, I aimed to integrate their lives more seamlessly with mine. I plunged into a new routine—before and after work, up and down the stairs to the apartment, twice daily for thirty-minute visits with Lillie, T.J., Perkins, and

Miss Tommie. I had sufficient time to feed them, wash their china dishes (paper plates were out of the question), scoop their litter boxes, and play with them. Lydia and Leo were oblivious to my busier schedule, but Lucius took note of my increased absences. He watched me climb the stairs, morning and night, every step of the way. I worried that he would punish me when he smelled the scent of the other cats on my clothes. But Lucius refrained from punishment, at least for the time being, and for which I was immensely grateful.

You Gotta Have Art

In my daily comings and goings, I sensed that something was missing from the cats' apartment. They needed to be exposed to art.

After two years of "collecting cats," and of justifying this process as easily as an editor explains the essential role of acquiring manuscripts for publication, I was about to collect inanimate objects again. The apartment gave me another excuse for hyper-consumption, a renewed opportunity to acquire things, collectibles, more stuff. I considered writing a pitch letter to the executive producer of *Extreme Makeover: Home Edition*, asking if the expert corps of builders, decorators, and carpenters assigned to the popular TV show could help me create the ideal home for four cats. I was afraid that the inquiry would be filed under "nutcase." I was serious, though, and also reflected on how much I had absorbed through osmosis at the museum by watching the curators install their collections and mount exhibitions. I was qualified to curate the cats' apartment, taking the art of feline living to a higher form.

I chose an obvious decorating theme. I went antiquing—just like in my B.C. (Before Cats) period—and found Victorian stereoscopic views of cats. I advanced to twentieth-century collectibles and bought mid-century mugs decorated with stylish "cool cats" and contemporary posters of cats in repose. And what would a full-out cat-themed decor be without an authentic Kit-Cat clock, ticking away the hours of the day? Did anyone say eclectic?

I wondered what Dr. Marzio—the museum's ultimate arbiter of taste— would say, he who was known for a counterintuitive style of exhibition installations. Art critics meant this as a compliment, and I went one better in thinking my boss simply had "The Marzio Touch," recognizing what works belong together even when they come from different continents, genres, and time periods—essentially a "Strangers in the Night" approach that worked every time Dr. Marzio walked into the museum's galleries and took charge of an installation. I had many opportunities to study at the hand of the master, though his purely minimalist, ultra-refined philosophy of art was not evident in my installation for the cats. I had to guess that he would have pat me on the back, said "thatta Cat Lady," and told the curators that they should be thankful I had not pursued their specialized line of work.

Nonetheless, I smiled every time I entered the apartment. Not only was I glad to see Lillie, T.J., Perkins, and Miss Tommie, but I also was pleased with how everything had come together visually. At least the colors and the textures were in sync, "dialoguing," as a curator would say favorably. Best of all, the four cats were living in harmony, and I hoped that their customized surroundings had a little something to do with the feelings of motherly, brotherly, and sisterly love. Whenever I left the apartment each morning and night, I said to no one in particular: "I love you."

On Demand

Perhaps Linus had been spying on Lillie, T.J., Perkins, and Miss Tommie all along, because almost as soon they were ensconced in the apartment, he became comfortable living in our backyard. Tom was showing up only once a week, and we couldn't justify leaving food and water bowls outside on an all-day, all-night basis to please one roving cat. There was no need for Linus to beg. We rushed to his side, feeding on demand.

One morning when Tom reappeared and ate beside Linus, Michael and I rearranged the pieces of the feline puzzle. Seeing the two cats together was an eye-opener. Their large, trademark-tomcat heads were shaped the same; their eyes were the identical color of green; and their large paws were disproportionate to their low-to-the-ground, small frames. Tom was Linus's father. Linus, the son of the almighty Tom, should be able to stand up to any cat, including Lucius. As soon as I started thinking along these lines, I stopped myself. We absolutely, positively could not adopt another cat. I saw Lucius glaring at me, daring me to defy my vow of abstinence.

Linus intensified his charms early in the month of May. We could pick him up easily and pet him from head to toe, and he reciprocated our affection. He liked to show off, wiggling and flipping on the back deck; the ugly duckling had become adorable. Michael and I decided to take Linus to get his proper veterinary tests and shots. Assuming he was healthy, we would find him a permanent home. I still had not revealed to Michael the outcome of my dream.

While Linus became a permanent fixture in our backyard, Tom continued to be unpredictable. Sometimes he waited for us in the morning, sometimes at night. We had focused so much attention on and channeled our energy toward relocating Lillie and her family that we had not given Tom his proper due.

Michael talked about trapping Tom so that we could have him neutered and try to give him a better life.

Tom disappeared forever in late April, and without telling us. The last time I saw him, he was climbing the stairs to the apartment to look inside. Was he saying goodbye to his family? Was he leaving because he was ill, retreating to die privately? I think the underlying message in Tom's vanishing, which was not an act, was that time was not conveniently on our side. We were approaching the one-year anniversary of Acorn's death, and then suddenly we lost another cat. Yet the circle of life continued unbroken with Linus. Did he adopt us, or did we handpick him?

We never learned the fate of Tom, and we have only one photograph of him—reclining on the cobblestones at the rear of our backyard—to stoke our memories. Often when I look at this photo, I am reminded of art collectors' stories of the one object that got away. But Tom was not an object, and to this day, Michael and I remember him as the one cat who never made it on our watch. I wish Tom would come back, not to free us from our guilt trips, but to give us another chance to help him.

We could save Linus from becoming another statistic published in the feline actuarial tables, which list three years old as the average life span for an outdoor tomcat. When Michael came home late one night after attending Houston's annual offshore technology conference, I heard him open the backyard gate and start talking to someone, and that someone was Linus. "What are you doing, little fella? Didn't Mommy feed you already?" "Now, wait a minute, Michael," I exclaimed as I opened the back door. "I am *not* his mommy." "Not yet," I murmured.

Command Performance

Maybe Michael heard my "not yet" comment, or maybe he had made up his mind to adopt Linus while driving home that night. Or Michael decided to keep Linus the moment he first saw him. It doesn't matter. When Michael opened the back door, Linus walked right in, as if he owned the joint. He raised his fluffy tail in a sign of victory. The "little kitten who could" had enticed Michael and me for good. Linus has never looked back since.

We sequestered Linus overnight in anticipation of his trip to the veterinarian's office. In keeping with his paranoid personality, Lucius was suspicious of the surreptitious and frenetic activity in our household. I made a small pallet for Linus on the sunporch that adjoins our bedroom, from where Lucius predictably tried to look underneath the door. Lydia initially feigned disinterest, whereas Leo was openly curious.

Apps for Cat Ladies

I need to head to Silicon Valley and meet someone who can help me develop what I think will make a great app. It's called the Catnapp©, and here's how it works. I'll find a stray cat (that is not a note to self, merely a given) and point my iPhone camera toward outlying streets in my neighborhood. The Catnapp© will quickly identify a fellow Cat Lady who will rescue the cat. Just imagine: All of this activity unfolds on my handheld screen.

I rescued our ten cats before the iPhone existed. Because the cats and I are so clearly meant for each other, the Catnapp© would not have been necessary in my rescue missions. But I am convinced that technology and Cat Ladies can make beautiful music together.

I peeked at Linus sleeping soundly through the night. Dr. O. had once told me that, almost immediately after a stray cat moves indoors, the cat will experience the best sleep of his or her life. Sleep and safety converged for Linus as he spent his first night with a roof over his head. Dr. O. was in the process of establishing a new clinic, and she referred me to a veterinary colleague at another nearby office.

The veterinarian's office obliged when I called the next morning to explain that "We had another." I briefly elaborated on this plain-spoken declaration, although there was not a whole lot to say. Yes, we had another, and who's counting? The vet techs fell in love with Linus's sweet disposition, but they were concerned that Linus's body was so tiny, and still so relatively weak, that he might not have enough blood to give for the critical tests. But Linus was brave and gave just enough. We were elated when the results came back negative and Linus was discharged with a clean bill of health.

This time when we arrived home, Lucius was waiting for us at the back door. Linus was still inside the carrier, so I knew that Lucius—if inclined—could not harm him. But Lucius also has a way of inflicting harm without physical injury. In a previous life, he must have watched the Hitchcock classic *Rebecca* because Lucius was impersonating Mrs. Danvers. Lucius put his face next to the carrier door and kept staring, trancelike, at Linus. Lucius's contemptuous look would have scared anyone, and would have made Mrs. Danvers proud. Only now there was no Maxim de Winter to impress, no Manderley to fight for. There was only Catland to defend, and me—the object of Lucius's desire—to protect. I could almost inhale Lucius's animosity, and I sensed we were in for a long haul integrating Linus into our family. I would need to give Linus a room of his own for a while, even if that meant Lucius was lying in wait on the other side of the door, giving an Academy Award-winning performance for pouting.

Just as Lucius was obsessed with me, I was obsessed with tending to Lucius. I was becoming the ultimate Cat Lady, catering to his every whim while bemoaning his psychotic behavior.

Madwoman

I have spent the past twenty years obsessing over art books. Producing a publication is the hard-won result of an unyielding quest for original scholarship. Working on a book, whether for twelve months or five years, requires a descent of a certain sort—into a selected historical period—and a drive to discover all that is new about the art of the time. The arrival of the month of June caused me to wonder if I was descending into a form of madness, just like Mrs. Danvers or another delusional character in a book of fiction.

I was thriving at the museum—lots of exciting book projects to manage, including a landmark publication on the history of Japanese photography. Home was another story. When I left for work in the morning, I kept hearing the voice of a cat. This could not be the case because we had rescued every living creature that had come to our door, with the exception of Tom. Was I hearing yet another voice from a new cat who would entice me further? Finally, I saw a grey tabby cat in our backyard, and instead of reassuring myself that I wasn't becoming mad, I became unhinged. Dinny always preached "calm, cool, and collected," and where would this unbecoming behavior leave me?

I was afraid that T.J. had escaped from the apartment. But I looked again at the cat, this time very intently. The cat was a he, and he wasn't T.J., thankfully. The T.J. body double looked up at me in earnest, trying to read my face. "Meow," he said. "Meow, meow," he repeated.

I looked at the cat once again and could feel the corners of my lips turning up into a smile. I didn't have to open my mouth and address this cat who would soon have a name. He blinked at me approvingly, knowing that I would be his voice.

Seduced

L.B.

*U*pon closer observation, I realized that I had seen the grey tabby cat walking up and down the street in our neighborhood. When I looked at this cat with the enormously expressive green eyes, I was staring unblinkingly at the prospect of integrating another cat into our household. Although there is no such thing yet as reading a cat's paw to divine the future, I had a vision when I reached out to touch this cat. Okay, maybe my vision was a bit eccentric, as is often the case with an art collector, but didn't I have a right to fill the gaps of my own collection?

I gave the tabby cat an entire can of wet food and petted him while he ate nonstop. Now I knew why I recognized him. He had once worn a red collar with a little stainless-steel bell dangling from a nametag. I could go through the motions of knocking on some of our neighbors' doors to try and track down the owner of the cat, but I had already rushed to judgment, deciding that the person who "owned" him had no business doing so.

All of us have cherished possessions that mean the world to us, for a variety of reasons. Curiously, I had never thought of myself as the owner of our cats. Rather, I own material objects and work in an environment that worships the acquisition of art. The word "owner" when used as a bridge between a pet and a human being is accurate, of course, as well as binding legally. I prefer the words "guardian" and "caregiver," and, most emphatically, the moniker "Cat Lady."

Had the grey cat's owner deliberately or unintentionally reneged on a commitment to love and respect this cat? Did the owner wish to de-clutter, shedding possession of the cat just as someone awakens on a Saturday morning and rids a closet of hopelessly out-of-date clothing? I could only guess that the cat's needs were no longer relevant to the person who had first helped him at some point in time—helped him by feeding him and by taking the responsibility to have him neutered. Whereas the past might not matter to whoever once took care of the cat, another part of my life with felines was about to move forward.

On the Prowl

Without his collar and tag, the cat no longer had a name. I named him L.B., short for Lydia's brother, because in some ways he could pass for a male version of Lydia, only without her heavy dose of exoticism. Like Lydia, L.B. had a wide band of all-black fur running perpendicularly down the center of his otherwise all-grey body. He also had a highly intelligent, inquisitive face, marked with white fur around the mouth. His paws were even more enormous than those that are a defining characteristic of Lillie and her clan. When I tipped off Michael to our new arrival, he revealed that, on one extremely cold night in January of this same year, before we had spotted Linus, he had noticed

L.B. trying to stay warm on the doormat of a neighboring home. The residents apparently never took note of the cat about to freeze outside, and Michael had restrained himself from pounding on their front door, inquiring "are you crazy?" to be so insensitive to an animal desperate for warmth.

Michael had thought momentarily about kidnapping the cat and sheltering him at our house overnight. At last, he was admitting to being Crazy Cat Man, on the prowl, contemplating taking someone else's pet. But who was L.B.'s owner? We asked, and no one knew. A next-door neighbor commented, "He's smart, he's a survivor. You don't need to worry about him." But we worried often.

Michael decided that L.B. should stand for something more poetic and metaphorical than simply "Lydia's brother." L.B.'s full name would be Lawrence Benson Lovejoy, with Lawrence serving as a reference to the nomadic Lawrence of Arabia, and Benson an affectionate nod to Lydia's given middle name.

Up on the Housetop

Michael and I could not keep L.B. at ground level. He preferred late-night assignations and arrived close to the stroke of 12:00 midnight to sleep on the lowest overhang of the roof.

L.B. summoned us early each morning with a full octave of meows, sounding like a tenor warming up his vocal chords before an operatic performance. Michael dutifully rushed downstairs and out the back door, calling "L.B., L.B., it's time for breakfast." Meanwhile, Linus was ensconced upstairs in the room that used to function exclusively as a sunporch and had become, thanks to the can't-say-no-to-cats couple, a toy-laden tree house with a panoramic view of our and our neighbors' backyards. Linus became very excited every time he saw L.B. on the other side of the windows, peering at his private lair. I wondered if the two had ever encountered each other when they wandered the streets, in search of food and companionship. I wondered, too, if they might get along if reunited inside. "Don't go there," said the suppressed voice of reason, still trying to overcome an ostensibly unstoppable force.

Before we could say meow, the awful sound of Linus's caterwauling filled the house. I tried sleeping with a pillow over my head; it was already a challenge to position the pillow so as not to mess up my hair. One night I couldn't take the noise any longer. I threw the pillow on the floor forcefully and yelled "STOP IT." I don't know where this deep, loud voice came from. We should have had Linus neutered immediately when we took him for his first checkup. But he was so physically delicate and weak, and we could not wait to bring him home and get him settled indoors. Neutering could wait, or so I had thought.

The Scoop on...

Being Prepared for Your Cats

Wearing your heart on your sleeve is one thing. Wearing a uniform is another. In spite of my full-time desire to care for cats, I have not gone so far as to have a laundered uniform hanging in my closet, some kind of special suit for a Cat Lady's pursuits. What I do advise, though, if you are inclined to feed stray cats on a regular basis, is that you buy trousers, or sweatpants, or shorts that come with deep pockets. Here's why.

Just as AAA advises drivers to store a spare tire in the trunk of a car, I recommend keeping a can of wet cat food in one pocket of a pair of pants (or shorts). I also fold a small paper plate, origami style, and store it in the other pocket. I am prepared to feed a hungry cat anytime. I used to carry a fork as well, especially if I was wearing pants with a back pocket, but I kept jabbing myself in the rear end.

The grilled foods for cats do not spoil as quickly as the ones labeled "gourmet chicken" or "cod, sole, and shrimp." I like to think of a "spare" can of cat food as the Cat Lady's equivalent of champagne on ice. There is always cause for spontaneous celebration when helping a cat in need.

p. 113: Bettina Rheims, French, born 1952, *Cat, Portrait of Back*, 1982

Brassaï, French, born Hungary, 1899-1984, *Untitled*, c. 1950

Brassaï, French, born Hungary, 1899-1984, *Vagabond Cat (Chat Vagabond)*, 1946

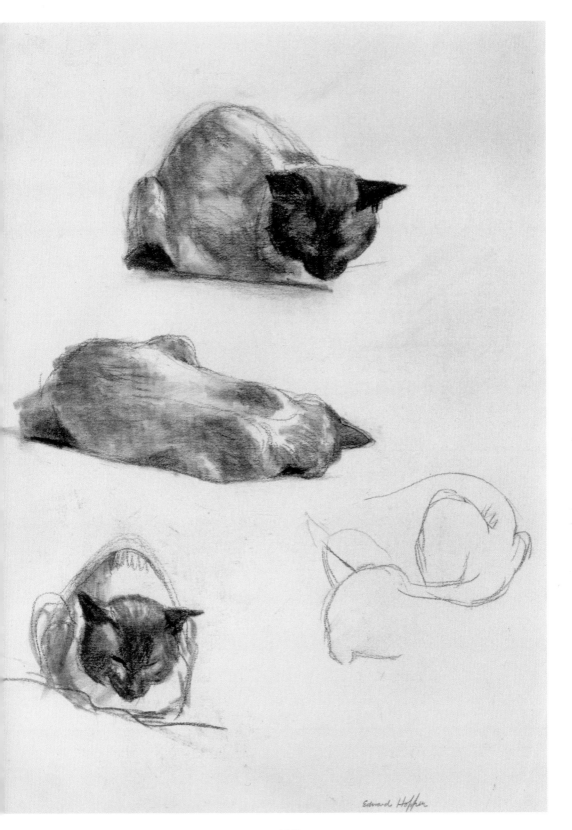

Edward Hopper

Théophile Alexandre Steinlen, Swiss, 1859–1923, *Summer: Cat on a Balustrade (L'Été-Chat sur une balustrade)*, 1909

p. 122: Todd Webb, American, 1905-2000, *Left Bank Laundry, Paris*, 1950

Pierre Bonnard, French, 1867-1947, *La Femme au Chat (The Woman with a Cat)*, c. 1912

Auguste Renoir, French, 1841-1919, *Woman with a Cat*, c. 1875

Frida Kahlo, Mexican, 1907-1954, *Self-portrait with Thorn Necklace and Hummingbird*, 1940

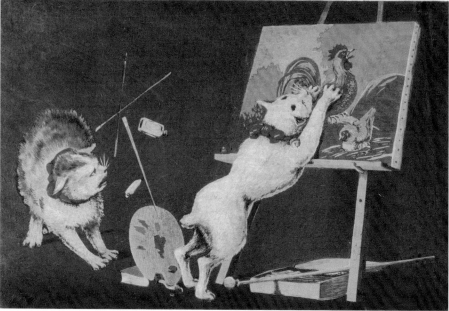

(top): Paul Klee, Swiss, 1879-1940, *Cat and Bird*, 1928

(bottom): Kobayashi Kiyochika, Japanese, 1847-1915, *Canvas and Cats*, c. 1879-81

Marc Chagall, French, born Russia, 1887–1985, *La Chatte métamorphosée en Femme (The Cat Transformed into a Woman)*, c.1928–31/1947

Dennis Farber, American, born 1946, *The Cat & The Kid*, 1991

Big-Name Artists, No-Name Cats

I always enjoyed reading William Safire's "On Language" column in the *New York Times,* especially when he regaled readers with tales from the "Gotcha! Gang." Editors often have a field day catching inconsistencies and pointing out glaring omissions. I focus on the language used to describe artistic creation, and a point of entry is often the title of a work of art. Perhaps something is in the water (or the meow mix) because I routinely find images of artworks whose titles leave a lot to be desired.

Pablo Picasso did not appear to have any difficulty keeping his mistresses straight, yet in many of his paintings of Dora Maar, he chose not to cite the name of the cat held by his mistress–muse. Alice Neel's granddaughter, Victoria, surely had named the cat she held somewhat awkwardly in a portrait painted of her with her pet. A calico is always a female cat, and I wonder if the notoriously opinionated Ms. Neel disapproved of the cat's name? Could the name have been too conventional for the nonconformist artist? And then there is a quiet image by Otsuji Kiyoji of photographer Ishimoto Yasuhiro on the streets of Kyoto, Japan. As Mr. Ishimoto approaches the lens of his tripod camera, a nameless white cat (though wearing a collar, hence presumably belonging to someone) studies the artist setting up his shot. What's with these big-name artists and no-name cats? Although it's impossible to rewrite history, editors and Cat Ladies can make the case for equal naming opportunities for artists and felines.

Dial "N" for Neuter

There should be a 24/7 hotline available for a Cat Lady to call whenever the mating calls of a cat become the dominant sounds of a household. Back in the 1970s, when I interned for the *Chicago Sun-Times,* I always jumped to perfect-posture attention whenever the chief copy-editor hollered "Get Me Rewrite." I found myself longing at home to shout, "Get Me Neuter." After enduring numerous sleepless nights, I speed-dialed Dr. O.'s number. Construction of her clinic was still not complete, and I panicked. Even though I thought I had equipped our house for every possible scenario involving cats, I had not set up a table for surgical procedures. And, unlike at nail salons, "walk-ins welcome" is not a customary front-door sign at a veterinary clinic. Just one day after my meltdown, I was relieved to secure an appointment for Linus to be neutered at the "standby" clinic recommended previously by Dr. O.

The night before Linus's neutering was interminable. All I could do was to stare bleary-eyed at the face of the clock until 7:00 a.m. mercifully arrived. Michael was wise to sleep downstairs, out of earshot of Linus making whoopee.

Linus wore himself out from his nocturnal celebrations, so much so that he cooperated when we placed him in the carrier that had transported so many of our cats to new places and ultimately new lifestyles. It was difficult not to think of Acorn, our only cat who had not survived the final leg of his journey. But as I was driving, I comforted myself with the thought that, with Linus and now L.B., too, we were beginning another chapter of feline living—and the work was purely nonfiction.

The vet techs oohed and aahed and cooed when they saw Linus again. He was healthier and fatter than when they had first met him, and Michael and I were like starry-eyed lovers, infatuated with Linus, who was too busy staring at the colorful fish gliding in the office aquarium to pay attention to his goofy parents.

How Dare You?

When Michael and I returned to retrieve Linus, he was waiting in his carrier, positioned near the receptionist's desk. He was not smiling. I wondered if he was groggy, a little out of it; or was he experiencing post-op resentment? During the car ride home, we found out fast that he was mad. Linus sprayed to ensure that the depth of his wounded feelings was known. Sure, it takes some time for a male cat's hormones to diffuse following the neutering procedure. The aftereffects had never been an issue for T.J., Leo, and Acorn, but from the intensity of the foul smell wafting from the carrier, Michael and I joked that Linus must have had enough hormones in his little body to last a lifetime. I lunged for the remote window buttons to let some fresh air into the car. The air-conditioning system was circulating, not masking, the overpowering odor. "How dare you?" Linus seemed to say as he frowned at me. "How dare you?" I retorted, sticking my tongue out like a child.

Cat Burglar

L.B. was waiting on the back deck when the three of us arrived home. We were surprised to see him at this hour, well before midnight. Had L.B. watched us take Linus to our car and worried about his fate? Or had he understood that we were taking care of Linus, and that if he hung out long enough, we would take care of him forever, too?

The brutal heat of late July arrived on cue, and when it reaches 100° Fahrenheit, I limit my time outdoors. But being a mere sweaty mortal was unavoidable because it was imperative that I interact often with L.B. to feed him. He also rather enjoyed my company. The question became one of how to help L.B. and suppress my hot flashes simultaneously.

The month of July also brought my forty-seventh birthday, and I thought seriously about giving myself a present that I could never buy in a specialty store. I wanted L.B. I didn't need to justify why I wanted him, and I wasn't competing with anyone to win his affection. L.B. also did not require validation, like an artwork that survives the curatorial filtering process and is acquired by a museum. I wasn't looking to possess L.B.; our house was filled with collectibles and knick-knacks that I had admired, sought, and bought. L.B. had possessed me, seduced me into believing that we could successfully add another cat to our family without missing a beat. The only sticking point was that unfortunate legal matter of ownership. I knew that L.B. still belonged technically to someone else in our neighborhood, although that unidentified person never posted a sign about a missing cat or made any aggressive effort to reclaim him.

I conferred with Linda, one of my best friends and an attorney whose practice had focused on family disputes. Linda was familiar with the evolution of our feline family, yet even she looked startled when I divulged the reason for our meeting. Linda knew me to be a law-abiding citizen—someone who returned library books on time, deposited nickels and dimes into the parking meter obediently, and filed for income taxes ahead of the annual April 15 deadline. Why was I seeking her expert advice on my legal rights as a cat burglar?

"Allow me to state my case," I said to the counselor-at-law. "I have fallen in love with another cat, and I want to make him mine." I explained that L.B. was not lost, nor was he born under our house, like some of the other cats, nor had he arrived out of nowhere. I suspected that L.B. had turned his back on neglect, just as a person summons the courage to escape from domestic violence. Linda reminded me that a pet belongs in the category of property. On one hand, I would be apprehending someone else's property. On the other hand, I could argue in court that someone's pet was trespassing on my property. No worries: I could persuade a judge that, despite taking the law into my own hands, I was not a danger to society. I jokingly asked Linda if I would need to enter a witness protection program if I stole L.B. My sympathetic friend, a totally by-the-book attorney, looked at me over her reading glasses. Nothing reeked of legalese in her response: "Nah."

I was so elated after meeting with Linda that I wasn't prepared for Michael's curt reaction when I shared my news. "You can't do this. He belongs to someone else," he said with unmistakable concern in his voice. "Oh, yes we can!" I responded confidently, long before Barack Obama made that phrase a rallying cry heard 'round the world. I turned around and went back outside to call L.B., who emerged from what I hoped was a cool hiding place underneath our house. "Come with me," I said theatrically.

Fast Friends

I was running out of space upstairs in which to initially sequester cats as we adopted them one by one. Lucius, Lydia, and Leo had free reign of the entire house, and Linus remained in seclusion on the sunporch. I gave L.B. a spare bedroom that Michael fondly calls the "Expedition Room" because its walls are covered with framed antique maps and *Vanity Fair* prints of Stanley and Livingston, and its bookshelves are lined with historical artifacts from Michael's numerous travels abroad.

L.B. was not accustomed to isolation. Living in a small space with four walls and a shallow closet was a big change for him, and he howled about his solitary confinement. But the room had two large windows overlooking the street— once L.B.'s main drag—and L.B. was inclined to monitor life outdoors from the plush comfort of a 1930s-era velvet-upholstered club chair. Before too long, L.B. began to resemble a lounge lizard, reclining leisurely and tanking up whenever his heart desired. Michael was angry about having a food bowl, a water bowl, and, most distressing, a litter box, in his beloved Expedition Room, although I assured him that this setup was temporary. "Give me a few more days to work out the 'intrafeline' logistics," I said firmly.

All of our resident cats understood that a new cat was in their midst. Lucius and Lydia hissed outside the door to the Expedition Room while Leo sat pensively. Was he about to meet another one of his half-brothers? Linus kept sniffing from behind the closed door of the sunporch, picking up L.B.'s scent from afar. Michael and I planned to introduce Linus first to L.B. Because of Linus's diminutive size, we assumed that Linus would not be a serious threat to L.B., and there was also the distinct possibility that the two cats already knew each other from previous hunting-and-gathering affairs.

Linus and L.B. never once hissed, spit, or fought, confirming our hunch that they would become BFFs. Linus was not related to L.B., but he could have been Bill Clinton's cousin. Linus has that same gift of backslapping bonhomie, effortless and exuberant. It was apparent that we needed to expand Linus and L.B.'s shared territory, so we closed off our bedroom again, letting the two new buddies form a kitty conga line that danced from the sunporch through the bedroom to the Expedition Room.

Introducing Linus to Leo was painless. I didn't need to bring out my whimsical sketch of the feline family tree to explain to Leo that Linus was his half-brother. Given Leo's sensitivity to Acorn's death, Leo must have felt a familiar tug from his heart when he first saw Linus. The two hit if off instantly. Linus was the perfect gentleman and courteous host whenever Leo visited him in our bedroom. If Linus could have talked, he would have said, "Mommy, I've got a friend coming to play today, and we want snacks." Per Linus's request, I kept a vintage McCoy cookie jar—shaped like a cat, what else?—full of treats.

Not a Pretty Picture

Michael and I were not incorporated, which is to say that we had not opened a bed and breakfast for cats. Still, there were innumerable factors to consider in re-upping our cat kingdom, recalibrating our lives to take care of five cats in our house, two of which were in separate quarters, and all the while maintaining a fixed schedule for helping the four cats who cohabitated in our garage apartment. We were not fully aware that, by expanding the playrooms and sleeping spaces for Linus and L.B., we were boxing ourselves into an exceedingly tight corner. What was I thinking in restricting Lucius's access to our bedroom, more specifically the conjugal bed where Lucius could sleep next to me at night and hold me tight?

Anyone spying on Michael and me in our house, on the watch for cats, would have suggested we commit ourselves voluntarily. We weren't glamorous subjects for the Houston-based paparazzi who cover movie and TV celebrities in town, but we could have mildly entertained a neighborhood voyeur who owned a decent pair of field binoculars. Most of our time at night was spent opening and closing the doors to the second-floor rooms; Michael was running around in his underwear, and I was directly behind him, wearing only my nightgown. Too bad Michael could not pass for a Calvin Klein model, or I a Victoria's Secret lingerie hottie.

Michael rarely obeyed my cardinal rule of opening the various doors gently to divert unnecessary attention from the territory under lock and key. He also had a bad habit of forgetting to shut the door to the Expedition Room, coming or going. As soon as I heard Lucius howling, I stopped whatever I was doing and hurried to what was once Michael's sanctum sanctorum to save L.B. and Linus from their unwanted fate.

We accepted that Lucius was certifiably nuts, at least in the annals of feline psychology, and anything relating to the Big D—Denial—fanned the flames of his mental imbalance. The idea of the off-limits chambers in our house no doubt intrigued Lucius, who had the most highly developed feline mind of the bunch. But I was reluctant to take our chances introducing him to L.B. and Linus, at least just yet. Two against one was not permitted in Lucius's paranoid world. What was good for Lucius was good for the feline body politic.

Michael and I grew tired quickly of keeping everyone but ourselves happy. L.B. was dozing in the Expedition Room and raised his head in alarm when he noticed me take Linus into the bedroom and shut the door behind me. There, waiting for him with great delectation, was Lucius. I held Linus closely to my chest and lied: "Don't worry, sweetheart. He's a nice kitty. Let's sit down and play with him."

Linus curled up on the carpet, attempting to look inconspicuous. He would have been a fool to move. Lucius approached Linus, eager to inspect his new specimen, sniffing him from head to toe. He breathed heavily as he tried to fake him out, quickly overwhelming Linus physically and undoubtedly subjugating him mentally. I had never seen Lucius in this state of extreme meltdown, and the sound of Linus whimpering helplessly broke my heart.

After what felt like an hour, and was probably only a few minutes, I managed to pry Linus from Lucius's agitated grasp while calling for help. Michael was oblivious. He was watching a rerun of a classic bowl game featuring the Texas Longhorns, as he does maniacally, and with the volume turned up at full blast to create the sense of crowd excitement in a football stadium. When Michael finally came to my and Linus's rescue, he raised his voice louder than I had ever heard—except for cheering on the Longhorns—and chased Lucius downstairs. We had just rescued L.B. from neglect, and here we were harassing Lucius. We were ashamed of ourselves.

I also hoped that Linus would forgive me for my transgressions. I could hear Lucius moaning indignantly and essentially talking to himself. As I comforted Linus, I started plotting and scheming to outfox Lucius. Michael and I would keep Linus and L.B. sequestered for as long as Lucius was alive. If Lucius did not like Linus at first sight, I couldn't imagine that he would cater to the whims of the much bigger and beefier L.B. And knowing Lucius, he would live to be a very old cat, just to keep me on my toes. No wonder I treated myself weekly to cheap pedicures.

Michael told me that I was being histrionic and melodramatic, that "they're just cats, doing what they need to do," and we needed to be patient. I suggested then, with undisguised acerbity, that he, Mr. Know-It-All, might try his winning hand at introducing Lucius to L.B.

Michael approached the official meeting of Lucius and L.B. with a devil-may-care insouciance. I knew exactly when the meeting was scheduled to occur, and I pretended that I had no concerns, either. "I know how guys relate to each other," said my very own Big Guy. "I'll take it from here." I went to take a shower.

I have it on the Big Guy's authority that the tension between Lucius and L.B. was immediate and palpable. Lucius had ample time to seethe before he saw L.B. for the first time, and L.B. had a look that registered, "I've been waiting for you, too." Their friction escalated to the point that Michael was forced to open the door to give them a wider berth for their bench-clearing brawl. Even over the sound of water sputtering in the shower, I could hear the shrieks and growls filling the house. I pushed back the shower curtain and called for Michael. "Are you letting them kill each other?" No response. I tried again. "Hello, anybody home?"

I worried that Lucius and L.B. had attacked Michael. I grabbed a bath towel and wrapped it around me hastily while I ran downstairs. Lucius and L.B. were locked in a Sumo-style grip, biting and chewing and spitting out each other's fur, and tumbling back and forth in the dining room. Tufts of grey and orange fur fell on the hardwood floor in disarray. Crescent-shaped claws hit the Persian carpets. I removed my towel and waved it repeatedly, thinking I could break up the cats with a damp substitute for an olive branch.

Then, on second thought, I froze in my wet tracks. I had no business refereeing cats at war. I had succeeded herding curators, to a certain extent, prompted by Dr. Marzio urging me to use my authority more aggressively, to make the curators accountable and beholden to their promises of generating original content. "Get the monkey off your back!" he said, again and again. And I was considering getting in between Lucius and L.B., running the risk of one of them pouncing on my back? Of course, if I could win this battle at home, I would feel further empowered to rack up victories at the office, to morph into an editrix along the lines of Anna Wintour. Remember, I told myself, just focus.

A focal point of the dining room's decor is an ornate gilt mirror positioned on top of an antique bureau. I was embarrassed when I caught a glimpse of myself naked—far from the privacy of our bathroom and way out of context. Just as the cat fight was an ugly sight to behold, I was not a pretty picture, either. I was even more horrified when I heard the doorbell and saw a UPS delivery man staring through the front-porch windows.

Wine, Women, and Song

I pretended not to hear the bell ringing insistently and darted behind a door leading to the butler's pantry, one of the most charming vestiges of our old house. As I was crouching indelicately, I noticed that L.B. was blatantly fascinated by my nakedness. I am not exaggerating, and I wish I could write that I don't blame him for leering. But I was—and am—a realist. I was glad that L.B. did not appear to be judgmental about the difference between a well-toned body and one that had lost its aerobic edge approximately two decades ago. Or maybe L.B. was being charitable and pretended not to care. But he was looking me over very carefully, from head to toe, studying the folds of my slightly sagging flesh the way an artist scrutinizes an anatomical model before putting a brush to the canvas. Even though L.B. had been neutered, he was still hardwired.

My friend Heather's husband, Mark, had picked up instantly on L.B.'s heightened state of masculinity. I once needed to remove a partition from a wall in our house, and Mark offered to help. L.B. liked the look—the latent power–of Mark's tool chest, and when Mark opened it to display an assortment of drills, L.B.'s face lit up. L.B. ran around the room joyfully, responding to the shrill sounds that only men who love to frequent hardware stores love to hear. Mark commented, "You've got yourself a 'dude kitty.'"

True, no one could accuse L.B. of being anything but super-manly. "You the man!" Michael said to him often, abandoning any pretense of correct grammar and showering L.B. with fawning praise. Soon the two were sprawled in front of the TV to watch Longhorns football on Saturday afternoons, rivaling only L.B. and Linus as a compatible couple. I staged an intervention when Michael invited L.B. to slurp some Budweiser from a pewter tankard. The two of them looked like outtakes from a Dutch genre painting, in which a tavern full of bawdy and boisterous men hold their drinks aloft, about to imbibe. Michael was defensive, claiming that L.B. had expressed such keen interest in the sacred six-pack formation that he could not deprive the cat of sipping this nectar of the gods.

It's All about You

If L.B. was "the man," then what did that make Lucius? He continued to get into raucous fights with L.B. over who was in charge, and it was very difficult to explain to a cat with a fractured identity that he was and would be The Man, forever. I caught Lucius staring at himself repeatedly in the same ornate mirror that had reflected my bare state. As if L.B. wasn't enough trouble, Lucius was seeing double. Who was the orange tabby looking at Lucius? The more I tried to help Lucius understand that he was seeing himself—that's *you*, Lucius—the more I realized that figuring him out was above my pay grade. Dr. O. strived to keep a straight face when I told her about Lucius's wondering, "Who am I?"

Michael and I consented to put Lucius on prescription medicine, to give him a little pick-me-upper so that he might feel more secure about himself. I highly commend Fluoxetine, known pejoratively as "kitty Prozac," an antidepressant that Lucius will be taking for the rest of his life. Sometimes I wish that I could apply the costly transdermal gel ($45.50 a month x twelve months a year x the rest of his life) inside the inner lobe of my ear and, like Lucius, get a buzz of drug-induced euphoria. People make fun of me when I confess that Lucius is on the equivalent of Prozac, and I admit that the revelation makes for amusing cocktail chatter—whenever the kids let me out at night. But Lucius's mental imbalance is not a laughing matter. What is sadly ironic is that his brain is probably not much bigger than the size of a pea, but what a noisy brain it must be.

Fat Thighs and Other Curiosities

I never thought of L.B. as a brainiac, but I had ample opportunities to reflect on his manhood. I felt increasingly self-conscious taking a shower because L.B. stationed himself on the bathmat, awaiting my big reveal. He wasn't shy about peeking at me to catch a glimpse of flesh, and he cleverly used one of his giant paws to lift a corner of the shower curtain. My mind often flashed back to Art 100 classes at Wellesley and studying the iconic American painting by Charles Willson Peale, *The Artist in His Museum*. For this self-portrait, Peale pulled back a crimson fringed curtain to reveal a veritable cabinet of curiosities housed at the Philadelphia Museum.

No one at Wellesley—art historian or not—would believe the scene taking place in my shower. I was the curiosity. L.B. fixated on my breasts, stomach, and thighs. Usually, I hurried to dry off and fasten the ties of my bathrobe, before he could stare for too long and his eyes bulged at the sight of my standing in the full-frontal position. I tried to cover up my body parts gracefully, but I wound up looking like a bad version of Eve in a medieval woodblock print. Talking to L.B. appeared to humor him. "Say, L.B., do you like fat thighs?" Whenever Michael heard me teasing L.B., he tried to earn bonus points for being a considerate husband. "You don't have fat thighs, dear." I appreciated his support, but I wanted L.B.'s approval, too.

Even when I wasn't taking a shower, L.B. spent a fair amount of time in the vicinity of the bathroom. I suspected more and more that he was once a man, and I collected my evidence just as an art historian assembles signal images to present a convincing lecture series on a subject. L.B. liked to study Michael's morning routine of selecting his clothes to wear for work, then shaving in front of the mirror over the bathroom vanity, and then showering. L.B. loved the scent of George Trumper sandalwood and West Indian Lime cologne, which Michael always applied after his shower. There was also L.B.'s attraction to Michael's boxer shorts from Brooks Brothers, as well as the cat's weird fascination with the toilet, additional indications that L.B. was a man who resorted to stereotypical bathroom humor to get a laugh. L.B. used his head to try and bump the handle on the toilet to make it flush, and I swore that if he ever took a paw to the toilet seat and raised it, I would bet one of my paychecks that he was a man who had transformed into a cat—an inversion of the classic vampire story. If L.B. left the toilet seat up, case closed.

My girlfriends were readily convinced of L.B.'s manhood, beyond a reasonable doubt. During the first Christmas that Michael and I spent with L.B., we hosted a holiday cocktail at which L.B. made a beeline for our female guests. For his warm-up routine, L.B. caressed their legs, from the ankles to the knees. Just as I had wanted L.B. with all of my heart, nothing could deter him from pursuing babe prey. My girlfriends encouraged me to pull up a chair at the table for L.B. Instead of discussing the latest books we had read or the movies we had seen, we talked about the manly cat purring like a baby.

Yes, L.B. is a man trapped inside of a cat's body. Was he initially trapped by a kind-hearted person, which led him to graduate from the classification of a stray cat to the status of a cared-for pet? Did he feel trapped knowing he was different from other cats, different because of having human, noticeably pronounced manly qualities? I think he would answer in the affirmative in both instances, and the ultimate seducer of women had added another notch to his belt. I doubt Wellesley would have approved of my succumbing this easily to a man's charms, but I felt satisfied knowing that L.B liked this Cat Lady so much.

Chapter 9

Rescued

Alvar

o I wish that I had never seen the white-and-black cat with an Oriental face, the cat who trotted through our backyard with the briskness of a cavalry horse one April morning, in 2004? The left side of my brain was clicking rapidly, informing me that I could not embark on another rescue mission. I had promised myself that L.B. was the last one. But the right side of my brain as well as my heart were conspiring just as quickly, urging me to consider the plight of another helpless animal, and to let happenstance become destiny. Looking back, I now realize that the cat whom we know and cherish as Alvar Alexei Lovejoy arrived with a mission: to test the depth of my commitment as Cat Lady.

Alvar was only a year old when I first saw him, and his snow-white body was almost beyond the state of emaciation. What was remarkable, though, was that the circles of black fur that appeared on his body were so uniform in diameter that they could have been drawn with a compass. The hand of the Master of the Feline Universe, if there could be such a named artist, was at work in creating this potentially beautiful cat. He even reminded me a little of Acorn.

Might as Well Face It, I'm Addicted to Cats

Alvar's pitiful physical condition made me wonder if he could be saved from the brink of disaster. Yet I did not rush to Alvar's side immediately. I was reluctant to start anew, mostly from fear of putting Lucius over the edge, sending him off to the scary deep end forever. His prescriptive bliss lasted only so long each day.

I didn't want to tell Michael that I spotted another stray cat in our backyard because of his inevitable knee-jerk reaction: "Great, let's adopt him!" Michael did not know that I had been having private conversations with myself, playing both the spoiler and the contrarian. I wanted to keep rescuing cats because I *had* to; there was no treatment for this undiagnosed addiction, no medicine that a doctor could prescribe to keep my Cat Lady feelings at bay. Nine cats and nine lives had a nice ring to it, and adding a tenth cat would not necessarily constitute a storybook ending. I also was running out of friends who were looking to adopt cats. There were no social-media platforms then for spreading the word instantaneously that a cat needed a permanent home.

I secretly began feeding Alvar sporadically and soon began to feed him habitually, with a tray in hand—like a butler serving his liege—when Michael departed on a business trip to Finland. On one of his phone calls home to check up on me, he described visiting architect Alvar Aalto's most famous buildings in Helsinki. "That's it!" I thought. The stray cat with the exotic, elongated face, a hallmark of the Oriental breed, will have a foreign name. Naturally, Alvar was grateful for every plate of food that I placed before him in the backyard or the driveway, but he had a peculiar way of showing his appreciation. He hissed in between eating and scraping up his food, using his jaw as a rake so as not to miss a bite. Was Alvar picking up on my do-I-or-don't-I-adopt-him vibes? Was he forcing me to make up my mind about whether he could join our family?

I described Alvar to Lynn, a cat-loving colleague, and when she expressed interest in possibly adopting him, I breathed a sigh of relief. Serving as a foster parent for a cat would be another first for me, another part of the plan that I could not have scripted prior to the dawn of the new millennium.

Act Now!

When Michael returned from Helsinki, I went public with my previously clandestine operation of feeding Alvar. Predictably, Michael was thrilled to observe a new cat in our midst, but less thrilled to learn that I had made headway in finding Alvar a home other than ours. Several days after conferring with Lynn, I heard from her assistant, Penny. Both women worked in the museum's public relations department, and I was delighted with the referral. But I was surprised to field so many probative questions about Alvar. In my world, cats had come to the back door, and I had conquered. There was never time for grand inquisitions. Penny wanted to know Alvar's size and weight, the color of his eyes (light green), whether he had already been neutered, and so forth. But I knew how to get through to her and took a page from her book. I responded with a breezy news release about Alvar.

"Beautiful White-and-Black Male Cat Needs Loving Home!" was the headline that led into my first paragraph about Alvar. I described his world-class appetite, commented on his zest for living, and remarked on his attractive coloring, which captured the artistry of a black-and-white drip painting by Jackson Pollock. The release was loaded with praise for Alvar, which he deserved. I concluded the announcement with a bold-faced "Act Now!" How could Penny refuse?

She bit the bait, and I arranged for her to come to our house one Sunday morning. The weather report that weekend indicated overcast skies, with intermittent drizzle. The familiarity of a feeding routine had prompted Alvar to refrain from hissing at me, and I thought I could coax him inside easily. When the doorbell rang, I wasn't expecting Penny to bring her mother to meet Alvar.

The two women followed me eagerly into the mudroom, where I had set out a plate of marinated seafood morsels and emptied a complete bag of catnip onto the doormat. I opened the back door to call for Alvar, only to find that the drizzle had turned to steady rain. I suspected he was hiding under our house and would emerge once he smelled food. I smiled through clenched teeth and reassured the two ladies that Alvar was not a figment of my imagination, nor the mythical subject of what I considered to be a well-written news release (even though I was rusty and had not drafted one in twenty years).

I wasn't clocking Alvar's arrival, but after waiting about thirty minutes I offered to head into the rain to find him. "Alvar, come to Mommy." Even though no one overheard me, I should have slapped myself for this conflicted remark; I believe the correct term is "Freudian slip." Sure, I could keep Alvar and undoubtedly wreak havoc at home, but I had insisted that he would not move indoors with us—meaning all of us, the humans and the felines, and what seemed like a new breed that combined the two species. Was I a lady who loved cats, or a cat who had come back to earth as a lady? And what about my main man, Michael, aka Crazy Cat Man? Or, as Heather was fond of reminding me, Michael was the best scout a Cat Lady could ever hope to find.

Singin' in the Rain

My search-and-rescue mission for Alvar lasted only a few minutes. I spotted him hiding underneath my car. Crawling on the cracked and wet pavement of the driveway and sliding in between the car's muddy front tires wasn't terribly appealing, but I was determined. I could still change Alvar's life at a moment's notice: I had primed Penny, through superlatives, to give Alvar a home.

I lifted Alvar gingerly. Even though he had fattened up from his regular feedings, he was still on the lower end of the weight scale. As Alvar rested calmly in my arms, I thought that, if I never lived another day, I could count his rescue as one of the best things I had done for a living creature.

I knew then that I would keep Alvar. Just as an artist feels compelled to create a work because of intense personal necessity, I needed to adopt Alvar, and it was only a matter of time. But I pretended to want to close the deal with Penny, whereas Alvar didn't bother to play along. He had a mind of his own, which instructed him to hide behind the washing machine. Penny and her mother wanted to pet him, to test whether he would respond to their affection. I tried to lure him with a feathered wand and rolled my fingers in the catnip on the mat, stretching my short arms as far as I could to reach him. Alvar did not care. He may have been young, and his mental capabilities not fully formed, but he had decided he did not want to leave our home.

After repeated attempts to persuade Alvar to emerge from hiding, I suggested that we fold our tents and try again during the workweek. Penny adopted the language of negotiators and said she would consider this "offer," and that I would hear from her in another day or so. I pretended to be exasperated by Alvar's willful inactivity. "You blew it!" I said several times as I poked my head behind the washing machine, playfully scolding him, and purely for the benefit of Penny and her mother. They smiled, now rather wanly, and I showed them to the front door.

I was not surprised when Penny contacted me early the next day and explained that she "was not ready for a cat." What does that mean? I was angered by her unemotional, detached rejection of Alvar. Either you have an open mind and an aching-for-a-cat heart, or you don't. I called Michael to discuss what I falsely termed our "setback." "Tell me something I don't already know," he said. "You want the cat." I politely begged to differ and told him that I was pursuing a new lead already. I had contacted Rad, the museum's website developer, whose love of cats and dogs was matched by his wife's devotion to animals.

Leave Me Alone

Rad stepped up to the plate and said that he would be glad to help. He had adopted one of his three cats from an agency working out of a PetSmart store near his home, and he offered to foster Alvar until putting him up for adoption through this agency.

I worried that Alvar would leap from my arms the next time that I picked him up, especially to give him away to a tall man who was not Michael. So I started practicing for the eventual handoff. For several days and nights, I left a pet-carrier door open outside and set it beside Alvar's food and water bowls, with the hope that he would explore the fuzzy blanket I had folded inside of the carrier. Alvar was curious, though his curiosity always stopped short of compliance.

Finally, the appointed hour of Alvar's big adventure was upon us, and Rad arrived punctually to take Alvar away. Now I felt like a film director advising an actor where to stand and what to say when it was time for "Action!" "Over there, Rad, quickly—go behind the tree, so he can't see you." But Alvar saw Rad, and Alvar did not want to be a bit actor in my amateur film. Alvar wanted to call the shots, and he raced across the street to make a point. He defecated in our neighbor's front yard, not bothering to cover his waste. Although I couldn't condone this very un-catlike behavior, I was pleased that Alvar seemed to be saying, "Leave me alone, with her."

Rad was a good sport. I apologized profusely for taking up his time, and when I noticed on the back seat of his car all of the food supplies, bags of litters, and toys he had bought for Alvar, I offered to reimburse him immediately. "But aren't we going to try again?" asked Rad. I had almost blown my cover. "Of course," I responded. "I'll call to arrange a time that is most convenient for you."

When Michael came home from work that night, I recapped what had happened with Rad. Unexpectedly, I began crying. Michael thought that I was distraught over the mishap with Rad, embarrassed to have dealt with a professional colleague in an unprofessional, sloppy way. But I was crying from relief. I would have to keep Alvar.

Civil Disobedience

If Michael was surprised by my decision, imagine the reaction of Dr. O. "Oh, no," she exclaimed, "You cannot do this to Lucius." Actually, she spoke to me in much harsher terms, although always respectful because I was her client and had been one from the first day that she had established her practice. She and I sometimes joked that she could sustain her practice based on caring for our nine cats alone. But Dr. O. was serious, and firm: "I strongly advise against your adopting another cat." She reminded me of all of our conversations about Lucius, as if I needed to be reminded.

This was the first time that I had been reprimanded for wanting to adopt another cat. Was a good deed about to be punished? I needed Dr. O.'s approval, just as much as I needed Dr. Marzio to applaud the stunning books that the publications department was producing for readers to enjoy. The problem was that I could not edit myself.

Even though obsession is rarely characterized as a linear progression, I was hoping to program the focused part of my obsession to adopt Alvar and to proceed on a straight path, with a newly calculated total of ten cats. I was willing to defy our veterinarian, to run the risk of civil disobedience at home, all for the love of Alvar. Dr. O. certainly understood my feeling, yet I sensed when I completed my conversation with her that she had held back with this parting shot: "You asked for it."

The Reign of Terror

I brought Alvar to live inside at the beginning of May. Racing through the house as nimbly as possible, I had hoped that I could fool Lucius, that he would be sleeping and not notice me running barefoot (shhh!) with a white-

and-black cat in my arms. The second-floor doors to the bedrooms were no longer closed to denote the lines drawn in the sand at Catland. I thought that Alvar, like L.B., would enjoy the view from the Expedition Room; no more false steps in announcing a newcomer to the residents. Why couldn't I harness an editor's aptitude for sequencing disparate words and images to mastermind the complicated relationships among our diverse cats—bringing them together across sidewalks and alleys, across days and months and years? The answer was to take everything slowly.

The front-desk assistant at the veterinary clinic was perplexed when I called to schedule an appointment for Alvar. "You're bringing who, Oliver—who is Oliver?" I explained the origins of his name, requested that she register him properly under the rubric "Lovejoy, Number 10" (Dr. O.'s brand-new office would be responsible soon for all ten cats), and grabbed the next available time slot for Alvar's checkup and neutering. Alvar was surprised to take a road trip so soon after landing at our house, but he behaved beautifully at the clinic. When I returned the next day, the vet techs were smiling when they greeted me at the door. "He's a really good cat." I thanked them for validating my instincts.

My instincts were also correct in assuming that Lucius was about to launch a new reign of terror. Still, I had rehearsed everything in my mind, and this time I planned to follow to the letter, and by the book, the best practices for introducing a new cat to an alpha cat. The rub was that Lucius was so much more than an alpha cat. He was—and is—the kind of cat who gets under your skin and never comes out. And it turns out Lucius had an IOU up his furry sleeve: Indignity, Outrage, and Utter Disbelief.

He hated Alvar. This was fire-and-brimstone stuff, and there was no way of getting around Lucius's hostility. Dr. O. was right. We had asked for it. Bringing another cat into our house, not just for temporary shelter but for life, was the final straw for Lucius.

Even though I was accustomed to cleaning up the cats' hairballs almost every morning, and to falling asleep at night on a bed whose blankets were covered with the fur shed by our cats, I still considered our home to be our nest—a place of comfort, a respite from the daily grind at the office. But we had given over our house to the cats, and Lucius was hell-bent on destroying everything in sight.

He ripped velvet and linen upholstery to shreds, scratched leather seating severely, and clawed at the legs of chests and desks that used to have a distinguished patina. Worse, he urinated on every pillow, sheet, and cushion he could find, and I was spraying Glade's French Vanilla deodorizer with the same force I used to demonstrate a fire extinguisher during the practice fire drills at the museum (I was assigned one year to be the third-floor fire warden in my

The Scoop on...

Mind-Blowing Catnip

I have a vivid dream: I clap my hands and announce "Catnip Party," and all of our cats start dancing. The lights are low, and the music is turned up to a suitable decibel that causes their hips to gyrate rhythmically and their tails to wiggle with abandon. I am their dealer, turning them on to a drug that I know they shouldn't take for granted, but that I will dispense as their recreational turn-on.

I like to sprinkle catnip on plates and place them strategically in a room. I've tried the dousing-the-carpet approach, but it takes days to vacuum every last particle of the stuff. At first, I thought I could buy extra doses of the cats' affection through catnip. Now, I save it for special occasions. Given our number of cats, that means ten birthday celebrations, plus all of the observed federal and religious holidays.

Maybe I can get a new gig and become a catnip party planner. I offer twelve years of solid experience, and I know where to find the best blends.

office building—go figure). The stench in our house was bad enough, but the look in Lucius's eyes was scarier. I never thought that Lucius's kidneys were failing, but I did attribute his "free-fall behavior" to the apparent fact that he had lost his mind a long time ago.

"Oxy-Moron"

I began researching behavioral-modification products on the market and became overwhelmed with the wide range of supposed remedies. Shopping for these products is not the same pleasant experience as stopping on the spur of the moment at a fragrance counter at Saks Fifth Avenue and testing a perfume or two with a quick spritz to the wrist or the neck. There are no fragrance samples at PetSmart. But I was attracted to the persuasive product descriptions. "Extreme urination deodorizer" or "ultimate elimination treatment" got my attention. The guaranteed results made me hopeful: "Stains Don't Come Back." I also was curious whether there was a fast-acting difference between "Stain and Odor Remover" and "Odor and Stain Remover." "Fresh 'n Clean" was appealing, too, and I kind of liked the "'n," which would never make the cut in art-historical prose. But only a moron would have believed in the miracle solution sold as the "super-oxy-strength urine cleanser." As Dr. O. put it, "Lucius is peeing because he's angry as hell."

My always genteel Southern mother never used an indelicate word such as "pee." I had to wait until my late forties to learn that this word is basically *de rigueur*, the accepted shortcut to describing indiscriminate elimination. There is no point in couching the language in fancy terminology, so I started using the three-letter word with abandon. It felt therapeutic to say "pee," a lot. The dismal truth for Michael and me, and for our other cats, was that there was no cure for Lucius. He had made up his mind to be angry, and we have paid the price.

Tell Me Why

I started to resent Lucius deeply. At one point, I lost track of counting how many days I came home from work to find that he had done it again, saturating blankets and bedding with his pee. I was tired of spending evenings in the mudroom, loading the washing machine and waiting for everything to dry, knowing that I would be in the same spot on the next night, and the next night. I tried not to raise my voice with him, but my usual self-restraint escaped me. "Why did you do this? Why did you do this?" I asked him as I vigorously waved the stinky evidence in front of his eyes. "Why did you pee?" Lucius did not respond to this word, but when I changed it to "wee," he got it. "Stop weeing." He ran whenever he heard me shouting in frustration.

Still, the hardest part was that I considered myself to be Lucius's faithful interpreter. I understood him, his ups and downs, his needs and fears. Despite his destructive behavior, I never went to sleep being mad at Lucius, whereas the same principle didn't always hold true when I was angry with Michael. I was in tune with Lucius the same way that an effective speechwriter—no matter the topic—nails every assignment. Lucius had given up securing my undivided attention several years and nine cats ago, but he wanted something more from me again. He needed to know that I loved him no matter what, that I had his back. I resolved to keep Alvar out of Lucius's sight.

Perhaps Alvar could make friends with the other cats, and they would protect him from Lucius. When Michael and I first introduced Alvar to L.B., the meeting lasted about a minute. We couldn't restrain L.B., who nearly ripped Alvar into two pieces; such was L.B.'s brute strength. Alvar's introduction to Linus was equally painful. I suspect L.B. told Linus not to be friendly. Lydia had become somewhat lost in the shuffle of all of the male cats who had moved into our house, but she swore absolute allegiance to Lucius and did as she was told by him. Leo was our only cat who accepted Alvar upon first sight. Michael and I returned again to our personal theory of evolution and of Tom's vast influence in the neighborhood: Was Alvar Leo's distant cousin?

We could have spent time re-examining the family tree, but instead we kept asking ourselves this: How did we wind up creating this behaviorally challenged world at home? Through rescuing and adopting six cats to live in our house, we had inadvertently fostered enormous egos, greed, colossal envy, passion, competition, and controversy that only one other world I knew could match: the art world. But I wasn't looking to replicate the art world at my residence. I was intent, however, on advancing the art of feline living.

Bribe and Groom

Happily, in contrast to the friction permeating our house, all was love and peace inside the garage apartment. Lillie, T.J., Perkins, and Miss Tommie were content beyond my wildest dreams, and bribing them with catnip regularly didn't hurt. T.J. was never going to grow up and become a major intellect, but he wanted to learn how to communicate with me. I taught him a few words and phrases, and he still gets by with "gimme a bunt." I put my head down, and he answers with a bunt. There is much to be said for his refreshing outlook on life. Even the reclusive Miss Tommie was emerging from her chrysalis. Whenever I offered her the back of my hand, a variation on a high five, Miss Tommie licked me as if to groom me. To this day, she thinks I am a cat, and how could I ask for anything more?

A Wing and a Prayer

I didn't think it would be possible to achieve a similar autopilot status in our household, but I was ready to try anything to diffuse the turf wars being waged among L.B., Linus, and Alvar. The skirmishes and hissy fits were getting old. I suggested to Michael that we try sequestering the three cats to enforce solidarity and to let them live apart from Lucius, Lydia, and Leo. I knew Michael would not easily forsake the Expedition Room again, but I offered to give up my home office, too.

"Let me get this straight," said Michael. "You're going to give L.B., Linus, and Alvar two of our three bedrooms? You're crazy." I don't know why Michael thought I was crazy to want to establish our own West Wing. This was our best shot at restoring some sense of feline equilibrium, and we also could solicit people's prayers.

Stepping over and in between the three litter boxes and the six bowls of food and water stationed in the two bedrooms was akin to running a Navy Seal obstacle course. Only the hardiest will survive. I think L.B., Linus, and Alvar had so much fun laughing—however a cat laughs—at Michael and me that we can thank our clumsiness for helping them to forge their bond. Within a few weeks of their inhabiting the West Wing, they became "the three amigos." So my new daily routine went like this: Feed Lucius, Lydia, and Leo first; run upstairs to feed L.B., Linus, and Alvar; scoop the three litter boxes upstairs and the two boxes downstairs; proceed to the garage apartment and feed Lillie, T.J., Perkins, and Miss Tommie; scoop their three litter boxes; shower and dress for work; arrive at work; edit, edit, and edit; return home and repeat feedings; sleep and, just maybe, dream.

The upside of the hustle and bustle was that Lydia blossomed under duress. I had never permitted myself to dream that she could become thoroughly domesticated, that she would exceed my lowball expectations. Lydia found her ladylike niche watching me prepare for work in the morning, from applying my purportedly age-defying moisturizer to using my preferred power tools—a blow dryer and a flat iron. Femininity suited Lydia, at last, and whenever she gazed adoringly at me from her chosen spot on the bathroom floor, she made me feel like Mommie Dearest—in a good way. I used to take my ten-minute makeup routine for granted, but Lydia led me to appreciate some of the rites of being a woman. No boys allowed.

One-a-Day multivitamins, tailor-made for women, did not cure my fatigue, and rest was in short supply. After several months of living life in the divided fast lanes of our house, I announced to Michael that I was opening the bedroom doors permanently. It was time to integrate all of the cats, and Lucius would have to accept Alvar.

In my determination to be an artful facilitator, was I subconsciously inspired by a famous collector such as Isabella Stewart Gardner, who turned heads for the unconventional combinations of art that she hung on the walls of her home? She had a talent for assembling works in such a way that they encountered one another without jockeying for supremacy. Could I look at the forced cohabitation of Lucius and Alvar—two dissimilar cats from day one—and compare that pairing to one of Mrs. Gardner's jaunty juxtapositions of an Old Master painting (Lucius) with an Impressionist drawing (Alvar)?

Time and Again

Lucius's rejection of Alvar proved that the heavyweight would not tolerate the rising star. His rejection also posed a philosophical problem, and I struggled with the idea of giving away our first cat in order to accommodate our last cat. Although Lucius was six years older than Alvar, it was not as though he was a used car with excessive mileage, ready to be traded-in. Lucius wasn't an aging athlete, either, whose time had come to hang up the cleats, to retire from the arena in which he had excelled. I recognized that my idea was pure fantasy because I could never abandon Lucius. I also knew the reality: No one would take him, given all of his issues. The challenge would become one of helping Lucius to understand that I could not help myself when I adopted Alvar. I was motivated by love and had rationalized this purely irrational feeling, which had crept up on me through the repetitive act of feeding a stray cat.

The challenges persist with Lucius, yet, despite the wear and tear on our nearly one-hundred-year-old house and on our post-middle-age nerves, the years with him have flown by. There are new hardships that accompany the recent diagnosis of his diabetes. The fact that Lucius has a Walgreens prescription saving club card further obscures the distinction between his human and his feline qualities.

Lucius has developed an older-age penchant for Zen-like meditation, which he swears by every morning on a lime-green placemat that I bought for him at Target. And, according to the Tao of Lucius, felines in their senior years crave pat-downs, particularly the ones classified as enhanced pat-downs. Lucius doesn't understand the uproar over the TSA guards or condone the outrage over the upgraded, full-body scans at airports worldwide. Every stroke matters immensely to Lucius, and there is no such thing in his world as my lingering too long over the back of his head or in between the blades of his shoulders. He takes everything in, and I would expect nothing less from Lucius as he observes the passing of time. He must know that he is reaching the shorter end of life.

I try not to think about life without Lucius, instead yearning for his and my intricate bond to endure. The moral of this story is that Lucius and I found each other—a crazy cat and a lady who is crazy about him—and we will remain together 'til death do us part.

A Loaded Question for Cat Lady

There is nothing like a "drive-thru" lane for saving time, except when the person at the other end of the intercom poses a question that stumps the driver.

I needed to pick up a prescription at Walgreens one morning, and all I expected to hear was the amount due at the cash register. Instead, the booming voice, the "Wizard of Walgreens," inquired: "Are you related to Lucius?"

It turns out that I am not in the Walgreens system, but Lucius is registered because of being diabetic. The search by surname had revealed only one given name, Lucius, and the billing record for his insulin.

Am I related to Lucius? That is a loaded question. I am his caregiver, his guardian, his mother, his wife, and, of course, his Cat Lady. Was the Wizard of Walgreens ready to hear my addled response, amplified via intercom? The driver behind me began honking his horn impatiently, and so I kept my response brief.

"Yes, I am related to Lucius," I said, with a satisfied smile on my face.

Lost and Found

Before Alvar appeared on the scene, I wasn't an entirely lost soul. I had held responsible editorial jobs consistently and had managed our household efficiently. The only element missing was cats. Michael and I had thoroughly embraced our life with felines, the good times and the bad times, and we had learned to cope with the heartbreak of Acorn's death. Alvar's gift was on another level.

Alvar rescued me from being an absolutist, someone who obeys orders in spite of the entreaties of the heart, someone who is intractable and literal to the core. I am paid to be literal in my professional line of work, but I am under no such contractual obligation at home.

With our ten cats, I abandoned the editor's colony of one to become part of a feline colony. Through all of my years of editing texts about art, I gained experience seeing the world of art through the eyes of historians. Now, I see the world at large—not only that unique window into the world that art provides—through the eyes of cats. I got outside the box.

People often ask me, "How could you tell which stray cats to work with?" Let's just say that my heart never led me astray. I can't claim to be a member of the elect who has been tapped by a higher power to render services to animals. I didn't always have a sense of my manifest destiny. Nor did I anticipate "The Change" (the cat-generated one, not menopause) as a competent career woman should. But I embraced the challenges, per Career Management 101. The path is well lit for this late bloomer, and I intend to keep putting my calling as Cat Lady to good use.

Coming to Terms

My home will never resemble one of the gorgeous, flawlessly appointed houses featured in *Architectural Digest*, in which a library table is adorned with polished silver picture frames of children skiing and sailing and collecting seashells on a beach. The massive mahogany library table that I inherited from Aunt Susan is overflowing with picture frames, only mine are filled with photos of cats reclining, leaping, sleeping, and cuddling. Wellesley, Sotheby's, the Art Institute of Chicago, and the Museum of Fine Arts, Houston, prepared me well to match the color and design of each frame to the subject depicted. Our cats taught me about the big picture, expanding my definition of balance and proportion.

In coming to terms with being Cat Lady, I gained control of my true self. As Lucius asks himself in the mirror, "Who am I?" I still carry the Ferragamo tote bag I bought more than a decade ago and acquire affordable antiques for our historic home. It's hard to resist material temptations. But when it comes to the "It" item in my life, it is the interconnectedness with Lucius, Lydia, Leo, Linus, L.B., Alvar, Lillie, T.J., Perkins, and Miss Tommie. Connectivity means much more to me than a command center for communications, a site for bundling electronic interactions. People, pets, art, and books enrich our spirits and fuel our lives. When I think about all of the connections that keep me going, cats are always on my mind.

Although the instrument of language is imperfect, there are certain words that are written with such authority that they defy reworking, and an editor should call it a day. I thank our ten cats for helping me to construct the perfect declarative sentence:

I am Cat Lady.

Besotted

*I*was taught by my parents that great books last a lifetime, and I have earned a living pursuing this philosophy. Books are treasures, and it is gratifying to build a collection of them, to share a good read with a friend and a colleague. Just as great art stands the test of time, great cats—and aren't they all four-legged masterpieces?—live on in our memories, long after their days on earth have expired. My Cat Lady chronicles are intended to keep the voices of our cats alive and to honor their collective legacy.

Decade of the Cat

During the first ten years of the new millennium, which I dubbed my personal "Decade of the Cat," I had the privilege of meeting many cats who did not come to live with Michael and me at Catland but who made their presences felt. Even though Dr. O. had issued numerous fair warnings and counseled me to "just say no," I wasn't fully ready to withdraw the hand I was so accustomed to extending. I understood that it was not possible to adopt every stray cat in our backyard, but I also believed that I could still be on the front line, partnering cats with people. Try telling a besotted person otherwise. After our intense, four-year adoptive period, Michael and I rescued another seven cats. I gave all but one of them their names, and I found them their permanent homes. I also returned a long-lost cat to his family, and I humbly believe that I made one cat's Christmas dream come true.

I remember Dylan, a one-year-old brown tabby cat who had apparently lost his way in the winding streets of our neighborhood, never to be reunited with his first family. I saw Larramie and his brother, Caspar, one fall morning, hours before Michael was due to return home on a flight from London. As soon as I saw them—one a grey tabby cat and the other a pure white cat—I had a funny feeling that the British Airways pilot had written a message in the sky: "Attention stray cats, Michael Lovejoy is returning to your neighborhood. Prepare for rescue." Big surprise: Michael wanted to keep the brotherly duo, both of whom eagerly took a leap of faith early on, trouncing their fears and loving our attention. They also were exceptionally beautiful felines who were adopted easily (by another couple).

A few summers ago, I noticed a slightly bedraggled cat sitting calmly and trying to keep cool in the grass of our neighbor's front lawn. Because the cat wore a collar, I assumed there was a corresponding home. But the more I observed this cat, the sooner I realized that something was amiss. One night I brought out some food and reached for the nametag on the cat's collar, and I was glad to introduce myself to Milky Way. "Wait right here, Milky Way," I said. "I'll make a phone call and get you home."

Several hours later, Milky Way's parents arrived. They were touched by the voice-mail message that Michael had left for them: "We love cats, and we will take care of Milky Way until we find you." It turns out that Milky Way had walked several miles, from the most exclusive part of town to our side of town. The rougher life did not become him, but I still hope that the few hours he spent with Michael and me soothed his soul.

Big Girls Don't Cry

No sooner had I bumped into Dr. O. at the grocery store and assured her I was not on the lookout for strays than I saw a very weak cat virtually tiptoeing down our driveway and into the backyard. I called Dr. O.'s office and begged for mercy: "Forget what I said. I have to get a dehydrated cat off the street." Dr. O. couldn't say no and let me pay a reduced fee for boarding Brooke, a spirited two-year-old. I stopped after work every day to see Brooke, forming a bond so deep that I began to wish she would not be adopted from Dr. O.'s clinic, at least not promptly. Within a month of having rescued Brooke, I found her a wonderful home with an art historian who shares my interest in pottery—only she writes about famous ceramic collections, not cracked pots.

"We did it! " I announced in a falsely chirpy voice on the day that I needed to sign over Brooke's papers to her new Cat Lady. And then I did it, as I always knew I would: I started crying at the thought of giving up my loving and appreciative new friend. I apologized to Paul, the vet tech who had been assigned to the weekend shifts with Brooke. He said, "There would be something wrong with you if you didn't cry." I know that big girls don't cry, especially in public. But sometimes I can't help myself.

When Saint Goes Marchin' In

The morning after the 2009 Super Bowl when the New Orleans Saints brought home the gold, I discovered a female black-and-white cat hiding in the bushes of our front lawn. Naming her Saint was an automatic and giddy response to the Saints' victory, and I felt confident that I could find the young cat a good home. I may have been out of the game on a regular basis, but I would not require years of early-morning practice to get up to speed again. I dispatched "kitty flyers" via e-mail and imposed on friends to post announcements about

Saint on their Facebook pages. Why not take advantage of all that social media had to offer?

The online matchmaking system worked. Four people stepped forward within an hour to express interest in adopting Saint. I had the pick of the litter.

I don't know how surrogates do it, even when a woman is paid a ransom's fee to carry another woman's child. I fell for Saint in a big way and didn't want to say good-bye. I had already experienced a bit of withdrawal after relocating her from our backyard to Dr. O.'s clinic. I missed the markers of Saint's existence on the back deck: the food and water bowls, the catnip toys, and the heating pad for when the nights were unusually chilly. At the clinic, I told Saint that I knew she was ready for the next stage of her life, and that I was fortunate to have taken care of her, even briefly.

I asked Michael if he wanted to accompany me to Dr. O.'s so that we both could bid Saint a fond adieu. He said, "That's okay. We'll always see Saint in our dreams." This has proven to be true, and I continue to imagine the first evening when Saint went marching in to her forever home.

Great Expectations

I first met a Chartreux named Bleu while visiting Saint, who lived above Bleu's kitty cage at Dr. O.'s clinic. Bleu's story was especially tragic. His first caregiver was diagnosed with terminal cancer, a situation that forced Bleu to be relocated to another home and eventually to Dr. O.'s clinic for adoption. There I was at Dr. O.'s, cooing over Saint, and there was Bleu, rattling the door of his cage as if to ask: Will you take care of me, too? Whenever I visited Dr. O.'s clinic to purchase Lucius's much-needed chill pills, I noticed that Bleu was always looking forlornly at me. Dr. O. told me that people looking to adopt a cat kept gravitating to the kittens at her clinic. At six years old, Bleu was considered to be an old guy by prospective Cat Ladies who prefer younger men.

So when December 2010 rolled around, I decided to take matters into my own hands and find Bleu a home. Emily, a longtime museum colleague, casually mentioned that she and her family were fostering a stray kitten. I seized the moment. I suggested that if she was ever interested in adopting a cat for her two sons, and a new friend for her corgi, I knew of an orphan. Before New Year's Eve, I was elated to hear that Bleu had made himself feel at home in Emily's house. He had great expectations of his future, and I remain grateful for the kindness shown to him.

Ready, Set, Go

I have been lucky to fulfill dual missions in my life thus far. I was hired to help implement the museum's mission through publishing, and I appointed myself to rescue cats. In both cases, mission accomplished. What is my next chapter? That remains to be seen, though I am counting again on serendipity.

When it comes to cats, you don't have to be like me and adopt as many as ten, and rescue another seven, to try and make a difference in the world. There is no set formula. All it takes is one cat and one person, and everything else will fall into place.

Cat Ladies, start your engines.

The Scoop on...

Driving a Purrfectly Tuned Engine

Are kittens like a drug—addictive? Unlike a drug they are not hazardous to our health, but like a drug, they can be controlled. Usually, addictive behavior is self-destructive, whereas for me, rescuing kittens and cats has proven to be an unimaginable exercise in self-awareness.

Two possible solutions for other Cat Ladies "in distress": 1) Remove the sheer curtains in your home and install wooden blinds; keep them shut to avoid sightings of felines outside. 2) Wear a pair of Jackie O style sunglasses whenever you enter PetSmart. You'll look mysterious, and the oversized dark shades will make it difficult for you to see directly, or even peripherally, the overwhelming number of cats available for adoption.

I have not yet discovered a medicinal solution or a homeopathic lotion for treating my addiction to cats. I also do not intend to seek professional counseling. Happily, the engine that drives this Cat Lady is still running strong.

Can you hear the engine purring?

Outside the Box

Who Dat Cat?

There is the gentle purr of the engine, and there is the mighty roar of the crowd.

Maybe it's because I grew up in New Orleans, where the chant of "Who Dat?" is sung by all of the fans supporting the Super Bowl-champion New Orleans Saints. Or maybe it's because I think of cats as "fur persons," as May Sarton once wrote lovingly. Although it's grammatically correct to use "that" when referring to animals, I've always preferred to use "who." I refer to the "cat who" came into my life and altered my lifestyle. Make the singular plural: I mean the ten cats who changed my life.

The question of "that" or "who" was played out in e-mail conversations I had in 2006 with Robert Rosenblum, one of the most distinguished art historians in the field. He was coauthoring one of the museum's books titled *Best in Show: The Dog in Art from the Renaissance to Today,* and the copy-editor recommended changing every one of Dr. Rosenblum's references from a "dog who" to a "dog that." Dr. Rosenblum would have none of that and wrote to me, pleading his case. He and I engaged in interesting exchanges about the humanization of animals. We agreed that there was no need to apply any convoluted theories to the care of our beloved pets. He loved dogs, and he accepted that I loved cats.

I personally requested making a global correction in the *Best in Show* manuscript: Every "that" referring to a dog should become a "who" again, and the copy-editor accommodated the author's and my fundamental reasons for wanting the sweeping change. Dr. Rosenblum offered to buy me a year's supply of cat food as an expression of his gratitude.

Reminiscing about "that" makes this editor and Cat Lady glad.

ACKNOWLEDGMENTS

C *at Lady Chronicles* began when I accepted a dare.

In 2009, my good friend and publishing colleague Joan Brookbank dared me to try my hand at writing about the Lovejoy feline family. Whenever I traveled on business from Houston to New York, Joan indulged me by letting me talk over dinner about the ten cats who have graced my and Michael's lives. She commented often that she was struck by the distinct personalities of our cats. One wintry night, in between her myriad professional projects, Joan drafted a book proposal for me to consider. I give full credit to her, whose creative spark lit my fire. She encouraged me to write an evocation of a special moment in time. I am further indebted to Joan for her astute advice and writing critiques, and for her unyielding desire to see her dare become a book.

Michael stood lovingly by my side, and when I was full initially of self-doubts about migrating from editorial to "the other side" of the publishing fence, he urged me to persevere because he knew I wanted to write a group biography. Marcy was keenly interested and was her usual aggressive self—I mean this as a compliment—in promoting her sister's work to friends and colleagues in the legal, real estate, and television worlds.

At the Museum of Fine Arts, Houston, I confided in only a few colleagues— out of a staff of nearly 650—about my personal book project, and I would like to thank them for keeping my secret safe. Heather Brand, then-editorial manager, agreed to the potentially awkward role of reviewing her boss's writing. To my mind, "boss" is a nominal title because Heather required no supervision. She is a devoted colleague and friend. Mari Carmen Ramírez, the Wortham curator of Latin American Art and director of the International Center for the Arts of the Americas, championed my cause over mojitos, which made my self-imposed writing deadlines easier to swallow. Anne Wilkes Tucker, the Gus and Lyndall Wortham curator of Photography, was aware of my interest in cats long before I announced my avocation as Cat Lady. Phenon Finley-Smiley, Gwendolyn H. Goffe, Kem Schultz, Marty Stein, and Karen Vetter also offered their friendship. I am grateful for the support of my new boss, MFAH Director Gary Tinterow.

Other friends and colleagues in the publishing arena provided sustained encouragement. I wish to thank especially Patricia Fidler, publisher of art and architecture, Yale University Press; Daphne Geismar, book designer and principal of Daphne Geismar Design; and Barbara Sadick, printing specialist for SYL. I also want to thank Kathy Hamilton and Linda Wells, both of whom insisted, "You go, Cat Lady." My Cat Lady friends at the Blue Bird Circle—the oldest volunteer women's organization in Houston—also kept me going with their own memorable stories about their precious pets. Mary Moehn Langfeldt and Audrey Block, two of my closest friends from Wellesley days, are major motivators who come equipped with intelligence, energy, and a LOL-brand of humor.

acknowledgments

I am extremely grateful to Caroline E. Oeben, "Dr. O.," who is the owner of and veterinarian at The Cat Doctor in Houston. Dr. O.'s love of cats knows no bounds, and her intellect and empathy have been the "wind beneath my wings" as I took flight.

I met my publisher, Marco Jellinek, by way of an art book, which makes perfect sense. My dear friend and colleague Bernard Bonnet, book buyer at The MFAH Shop of the Museum of Fine Arts, Houston, gifted me with a copy of *The Well-Read Cat*, published by Officina Libraria. I liked the book very much and asked Joan if she thought that Marco's publishing house might be receptive to receiving a proposal for another illustrated book about cats. I thank Marco for believing in my story and for giving me the opportunity to paint a portrait of my feline family. My deep thanks go also to John Brancati, vice president at ACC Distribution, and Diana Steele, managing director of the Antique Collectors' Club. Jennifer Burch and Sudha Dunienville at ACC are terrific colleagues.

Kim Yarwood, a cat-loving editor, improved my manuscript with her perfect precisions. The Galleranis are true kitty whisperers: Paola for her elegant book design, and her mother, Gabriella, for her lovely pencil portraits. Serena Solla was always attentive and helpful.

When I learned that I would be published, my mother-in-law, Joan Taylor, and my sister-in-law, Penny McAuley, whooped it up.

I like to think that my professional mentor and personal role model, Virginia "Dinny" Butts, approves of this publication. When Dinny died, she bequeathed to me her cultured-pearl necklace. Dinny never kept tabs on reciprocating gifts, but I am augmenting one of her public bequests by donating a portion of my proceeds from the sales of *Cat Lady Chronicles* to the Virginia Butts Berger Cat Clinic at the Anti-Cruelty Society in Chicago.

In closing, I wish to thank my parents, Marilyn and Ed Planer, for demonstrating the depths of unconditional love. They did not know that their first child would grow up to become Cat Lady. Upon my revelation, they embraced me like a newborn. My parents' compassionate example inspired me in so many ways, especially in wanting to leave an imprint on the hearts of cats.

My father died a month before the final manuscript of *Cat Lady Chronicles* was due to Officina Libraria. Fortunately, I had seen him two weeks before he passed away, and I had an opportunity to tell him about the plans for publication. Ever the seasoned journalist, he chose his words carefully. Reacting to my news, he commented, "Great, I'm proud of you." I dedicate this book to the loving memory of my father.

Finally, I trust that I have made my feelings known about Lucius, Lydia, Lillie, Leo, T.J., Perkins, Miss Tommie, Linus, L.B., and Alvar. As always, they have the last word.

List of Illustrations & Photo Credits

All photographs of artworks from the Museum of Fine Arts, Houston, were provided courtesy of the Department of Photographic Services: Thomas R. DuBrock and Will H. Michels, collection photographers. Every effort was made to contact the copyright holder of each image reproduced in this book.

Cover, p. 33

Takahashi Hiroaki (Shotei), Japanese, 1871-1945; published by Fusui Gabo, Japanese, active 1930s, *Cat Prowling Around a Staked Tomato Plant*, 1931

Woodblock print, block: 20 3/16 x 13 7/8 in. (51.3 x 35.3 cm); sheet: 20 7/8 x 13 7/8 in. (53.1 x 35.3 cm).
The Museum of Fine Arts, Houston, Gift of Stephen and Stephanie Hamilton in memory of Leslie A. Hamilton, 2005.324

Endsheets, pp. 9, 21, 49, 59, 67, 79, 95, 109, 139, 153, 159

Original pencil drawings by Gabriella Gallerani

© Gabriella Gallerani

Title page and back cover

Diane Lovejoy and her father, Ed Planer, in Jackson Square, New Orleans, Louisiana, 1957.

Photograph by Joe Budde.

p. 6

Thomas Eakins, American, 1844-1916, *Cat in Eakins's Yard*, c. 1880-90

Platinum print on paper, 4 3/4 x 2 5/8 in. (12.1 x 6.7 cm)
Hirshhorn Museum and Sculpture Garden, Smithsonian Institution, Gift of Joseph H. Hirshhorn, 1966, 83.66
Photo © Hirshhorn Museum and Sculpture Garden, Smithsonian Institution

p. 34

Félix Emile-Jean Vallotton, Swiss, 1865-1925, *Laziness (La Paresse)*, 1896

Woodcut, block: 7 x 8 3/4 in. (17.8 x 22.2 cm); sheet: 9 7/16 x 12 in. (24 x 30.5 cm)
The Museum of Fine Arts, Houston, Gift of the Virginia and Ira Jackson Collection in memory of Virginia Jackson, 2001.527

p. 35

Ishikawa Toraji, Japanese, 1875-1964, *Tsuzure*, from the series *Ten Nudes*, 1934

Print, 15 x 19 1/16 in. (38.1 x 48.4 cm)
Brooklyn Museum, Gift of the estate of Dr. Eleanor Z. Wallace, 2007.32.9
© Artist or artist's estate. Photo © Brooklyn Museum

p. 36

Toshikata Mizuno, Japanese, 1866-1908, *Woman after a Bath (Married Woman of the Kansei Era)*, from the series *Thirty-six Types of Beauties (Sanjurokkasen)*, 1891-93

Woodblock print, ink on paper, 14 x 9 1/2 in. (35.6 x 31.1 cm)
The Metropolitan Museum of Art, New York, 1984.210.1-.72
© The Metropolitan Museum of Art, New York. Image source: Art Resource, NY

p. 37

Utagawa Kunitoshi, Japanese, 1847-1899, *Popular Hotspring Spa for Cats (Ryūkō neko no onse)*, Meiji era

Woodblock print (nishiki-e), ink and color on paper, 14 7/16 x 9 13/16 in. (36.7 x 24.9 cm)
Museum of Fine Arts, Boston, William Sturgis Bigelow Collection, 11.44665
Photo © 2012 Museum of Fine Arts, Boston

p. 38

Joseph Wright of Derby, English, 1734-1797, *Dressing the Kitten*, c. 1768-70

Oil on canvas, 35 3/4 x 28.5 in. (90.8 x 72.4 cm)
Kenwood House, London, United Kingdom
© English Heritage Photo Library/ The Bridgeman Art Library

p. 39

Wanda Wulz, Italian, 1903-1984, *Io + Gatto*, 1932

Gelatin silver print, 11 9/16 x 9 1/8 in. (29.4 x 23.2 cm)
Fratelli Alinari Museum Collections-Zannier Collection, Florence
© Fratelli Alinari Museum Collections-Zannier Collection, Florence

p. 40

Brassaï, French, born Hungary, 1899-1984, *Cat with Phosphorescent Eyes*, 1936

Gelatin silver print, image/sheet: 11 7/16 x 8 1/4 in. (29 x 21 cm)
The Museum of Fine Arts, Houston, Gift of Alice C. Simkins in memory of William Stewart Simkins, 98.8
© The Brassaï Estate-RMN; © Ministère de la Culture / Médiathèque du Patrimoine, Dist. RMN

p. 41

Ron Evans, American, born 1943, *Climbing Cat*, 1983

Gelatin silver print, image: 12 1/4 x 12 3/16 in. (31.1 x 31 cm); sheet: 20 x 15 15/16 in. (50.8 x 40.5 cm)

The Museum of Fine Arts, Houston, Gift of Clinton T. Willour in honor of Marjorie Horning on the occasion of her special birthday, 97.292
© Ron Evans

p. 42

François Boucher, French, 1703–1770, *La Toilette*, 1742

Oil on canvas, 20.7 x 26.2 in. (52.5 x 66.5 cm)
Thyssen-Bornemisza, Madrid
Kharbine-Tapabor/The Art Archive at Art Resource, NY

p. 43

Brassaï, French, born Hungary, 1899–1984, *Opium Smoker and Cat, Paris (Fumeuse d'opium au chat, Paris)*, c. 1931

Gelatin silver print, image/sheet: 8 11/16 x 11 3/4 in. (22.1 x 29.8 cm)
The Museum of Fine Arts, Houston, Gift of Alice C. Simkins, 94.382
© The Brassaï Estate–RMN; © Ministère de la Culture / Médiathèque du Patrimoine, Dist. RMN

p. 44

Unknown photographer, *Cat posed with Mexican Serape*, c. 1866–68

Ambrotype
De Golyer Library, Southern Methodist University, Dallas, Texas, Lawrence T. Jones III Texas Photography Collection, Ag2008.005

p. 45

G.T., possibly English, *Portrait of a Woman*, c. 1830

Watercolor on ivory, velvet, and glass, sight: 3 1/8 x 2 9/16 in. (7.9 x 6.5 cm); frame: 5 1/4 x 4 1/2 in. (13.3 x 11.4 cm)
The Museum of Fine Arts, Houston; The Rienzi Collection, Bequest of Caroline A. Ross, 2005.1630

p. 46

Marcus Stone, English, 1840–1921, *Il y en a toujours un autre*, 1852

Oil on canvas, 60 1/2 x 27 3/4 in. (153.7 x 70.5 cm)
Tate Gallery, London, United Kingdom, Presented by the Trustees of the Chantrey Bequest 1882, N01583
Photo © Tate, London 2012

p. 47

Yamamoto Masao, Japanese, born 1957, *Untitled*, from the series *A Box of Ku*, 2001

Gelatin silver print, image/sheet: 4 5/16 x 1 15/16 in. (11 x 4.9 cm)
The Museum of Fine Arts, Houston, Gift of Clinton T. Willour in honor of Betty Moody, 2006.160
© Yamamoto Masao

p. 48

Yva (Else Neuländer-Simon), German, 1900–1942, *Untitled*, c. 1931

Gelatin silver print, 8 1/8 x 6 1/1/6 in. (20.7 x 15.4 cm)
The Museum of Fine Arts, Houston, Gift of an anonymous

donor in honor of Diane Lovejoy and the publication of her book *Cat Lady Chronicles*, 2012.300
© Estate of Yva (Else Neuländer-Simon)

p. 113

Bettina Rheims, French, born 1952, *Cat, Portrait of Back*, 1982

Gelatin silver print, image: 11 5/8 x 9 11/16 in. (29.5 x 24.6 cm)
The Museum of Fine Arts, Houston, The Allan Chasanoff Photographic Collection, 91.1032
© Bettina Rheims

p. 114

Brassaï, French, born Hungary, 1899–1984, *Untitled*, c. 1950

Gelatin silver print, image/sheet: 11 9/16 x 8 7/16 in. (29.4 x 21.4 cm)
The Museum of Fine Arts, Houston, Gift of Joseph Chanin, 99.673
© The Brassaï Estate–RMN; © Ministère de la Culture / Médiathèque du Patrimoine, Dist. RMN

p. 115

Brassaï, French, born Hungary, 1899–1984, *Vagabond Cat (Chat Vagabond)*, 1946

Gelatin silver print, image/sheet: 11 9/16 x 9 1/4 in. (29.4 x 23.5 cm)
The Museum of Fine Arts, Houston, The Manfred Heiting Collection, 2002.701
© The Brassaï Estate–RMN; © Ministère de la Culture / Médiathèque du Patrimoine, Dist. RMN

pp. 116–117

Edward Hopper, American, 1882–1967, *Cat Study*, 1941

Conté crayon on paper, image/sheet: 15 x 21 3/4 in. (38.1 x 55.2 cm)
The Museum of Fine Arts, Houston, Museum purchase with funds provided by the Alvin S. Romansky Prints and Drawings Accessions Endowment Fund and the Marjorie G. and Evan C. Horning Print Fund, 2003.315
Photo licensed by the heirs of Josephine N. Hopper

p. 118

Winslow Homer, American, 1836–1910, *The Dinner Horn*, from *Harper's Weekly*, June 11, 1870

Wood engraving, plate : 13 13/16 x 9 in. (35.1 x 22.9 cm); sheet: 16 x 10 15/16 in. (40.6 x 27.8 cm.
The Museum of Fine Arts, Houston, The Mavis P. and Mary Wilson Kelsey Collection of Winslow Homer Graphics, 75.780

p. 119

Tod Papageorge, American, born 1940, *Cat and Surfer, Laguna Beach*, 1978

Gelatin silver print, image: 10 9/16 x 15 9/16 in. (26.8 x 39.5 cm); sheet: 14 x 16 7/8 in. (35.6 x 42.9 cm).
The Museum of Fine Arts, Houston, Gift of AT&T, 82.451
© Tod Papageorge

p. 120
Théophile Alexandre Steinlen, Swiss, 1859–1923, *Summer: Cat on a Balustrade (L'Été-Chat sur une balustrade)*, 1909

Lithograph in colors, sheet: 19 13/16 x 24 3/4 in. (50.3 x 62.9 cm)
The Museum of Fine Arts, Houston, Gift of the Virginia and Ira Jackson Collection in memory of Virginia Jackson, 2001.520

p. 121 (top)
Olive Rush, American, 1873–1966, *The Huntress*, 1942

Watercolor on wove paper, sheet: 15 x 21 11/16 in. (38.1 x 55.1 cm)
The Museum of Fine Arts, Houston, Gift of Miss Ima Hogg, 43.1
© Estate of Olive Rush

p. 121 (bottom)
Cornelis de Visscher, Dutch, 1629–1658, *The Large Cat*, c. 1657

Engraving, plate: 5 9/16 x 7 3/16 in. (14.1 x 18.3 cm); sheet: 5 5/8 x 7 1/4 in. (14.3 x 18.4 cm)
The Philadelphia Museum of Art, The Muriel and Philip Berman Gift, acquired from the John T. Morris Collection given to the Pennsylvania Academy of the Fine Arts in 1925 by Lydia Thompson Morris, with funds contributed by Muriel and Philip Berman, Gifts (by exchange) of Lisa Norris Elkins, Bryant W. Langston, Samuel S. White 3rd and Vera White, with additional funds contributed by John Howard McFadden, Jr., Thomas Skelton Harrison, and the Philip H. and A.S.W. Rosenbach Foundation, 1985, 1985-52-383
Photo © Philadelphia Museum of Art

p. 122
Todd Webb, American, 1905–2000, *Left Bank Laundry, Paris*, 1950

Gelatin silver print, image: 12 7/16 x 9 7/16 in. (31.6 x 24 cm); sheet: 13 15/16 x 10 15/16 in. (35.4 x 27.8 cm).
The Museum of Fine Arts, Houston, Gift of Robert Steinke, 2010.1950
© Todd Webb, Courtesy of Evans Gallery and Estate of Todd & Lucille Webb, Portland, Maine USA

p. 123
Pierre Bonnard, French, 1867–1947, *La Femme au Chat (The Woman with a Cat)*, c. 1912

Oil on canvas, 30.7 x 30.4 in. (78 x 77.2 cm)
Musée d'Orsay, Paris, France, RF 1977 84, AM 3721
© 2012 Artists Rights Society (ARS), New York/ADAGP, Paris.
Photo: Réunion des Musées Nationaux/Art Resource, NY

p. 124
Auguste Renoir, French, 1841–1919, *Woman with a Cat*, c. 1875

Oil on canvas, 22 1/16 x 18 1/4 in. (56 x 46.4 cm)
National Gallery of Art, Washington, Gift of Mr. and Mrs. Benjamin E. Levy, 1950.12.1
Photo © National Gallery of Art, Washington

p. 125
Frida Kahlo, Mexican, 1907–1954, *Self-portrait with Thorn Necklace and Hummingbird*, 1940

Oil on canvas, 24.1 x 18.5 in. (61.25 x 47 cm)
Harry Ransom Center, Nickolas Muray Collection of Modern Mexican Art, 66.6
© 2012 Banco de México Diego Rivera Frida Kahlo Museums Trust, Mexico, D.F./Artists Rights Society (ARS), New York. Photo © Harry Ransom Center, Nickolas Muray Collection of Modern Mexican Art

p. 126 (top)
Paul Klee, Swiss, 1879–1940, *Cat and Bird*, 1928

Oil and ink on gessoed canvas, mounted on wood, 15 x 21 in. (38.1 x 53.2 cm). The Museum of Modern Art, Sidney and Harriet Janis Collection Fund and Gift of Suzy Prudden and Joan H. Meijer in memory of F. H. Hirschland, 300.1975
© 2012 Artists Rights Society (ARS), New York. Digital Image © The Museum of Modern Art/Licensed by SCALA Art Resource/NY

p. 126 (bottom)
Kobayashi Kiyochika, Japanese, 1847–1915, *Canvas and Cats*, c. 1879–81

Color woodblock print, image: 9 1/2 x 14 1/8 in. (24.1 x 35.8 cm); sheet: 9 1/2 x 14 5/16 in. (24.1 x 36.3 cm).
Los Angeles County Museum of Art, Gift of Carl Holmes, M.71.100.66
Digital Image © 2012 Museum Associates/LACMA. Licensed by Art Resource, NY

p. 127
Marc Chagall, French, born Russia, 1887–1985, *La Chatte métamorphosée en Femme (The Cat Transformed into a Woman)*, c.1928–31/1947

Etching, drypoint and oil on paper, 11.6 x 9 1/2 in. (29.5 x 24.1 cm)
Tate Gallery, London, United Kingdom, Presented by Lady Clerk 1947, N05759
© 2012 Artists Rights Society (ARS), New York/ADAGP, Paris.
Photo © Tate, London 2012

p. 128
Dennis Farber, American, born 1946, *The Cat & The Kid*, 1991

Dye diffusion transfer print, image: 23 7/8 x 19 5/8 in. (60.6 x 49.8 cm); sheet: 27 7/16 x 22 in. (69.7 x 55.9 cm).
The Museum of Fine Arts, Houston, Gift of Karl Benjamin, 2000.670
© Dennis Farber